Rage in the Streets

Recent Books by J U L E S   A R C H E R

JULES ARCHER

Rage
IN THE
Streets

Mob Violence in America

Illustrated by LYDIA J. HESS

BROWNDEER PRESS

HARCOURT BRACE & COMPANY

SAN DIEGO   NEW YORK   LONDON

Library of Congress Cataloging-in-Publication Data
Archer, Jules.
Rage in the streets: mob violence in America/by Jules Archer.
p.   cm.
"Browndeer Press."
Includes bibliographical references and index.
Summary: A history of mob violence in the United States, from the
time of the American Revolution to the riots in Los Angeles in 1992.
ISBN 0-15-277691-5
1. Violence—United States—History—Juvenile literature.   2. United States—Social
conditions—Juvenile literature.   [1. Riots—History.   2. Violence—History.
3. United States—Social conditions.]   I. Title.
HN90.V5A73   1994
303.6'0973—dc20   93-5710

Designed by Camilla Filancia
Printed in the United States of America
First edition   A B C D E

To my granddaughters,

KIRSTEN, COLLEEN, ERIN, *and* ZOË

CONTENTS

Introduction 1

Mobs Driven by Passion   3
The Psychology of Mobs   4
"The Cost of Neglect of the
    Last Twenty-Five Years"   5

**1. When Court Decisions
   Trigger Violence 9**

"A Little Rebellion Now
    and Then"   11
"Get a Rope! Lynch Her!"   13
School Buses Dynamited   16
The Rodney King Case   17
"The City Went Wild"   18
"We Are Sitting on a Powder Keg"   21
Operation Rescue   23

**2. When Intolerance Leads
   to Violence 27**

"Down with the Convent!"   28
The Convent Is Stormed   29
"A Base and Cowardly Act"   30

Persecuting the Chinese   32
Barring Chinese Immigration   34
"Murdered by a Mob"   36
"Hang the Jew!"   37
Wartime Hysteria   38
The Palmer Raid Riots   40

**3. When Racial Prejudice
   Creates Violence 45**

"They're Going to Hang Him!"   47
When Enslaved
    Blacks Rioted   48
The Ku Klux Klan   50
Race Riots in the North   50
Chicago Beaches—Blacks
    Keep Out!   52
Racial Hatred and Lynchings   53
The Zoot-Suit Riots   54
Detroit's "Bloody Week"   54
Lynching African-American
    Veterans   56
The Freedom Riders Risk
    Their Lives   59
"Racism in the First Degree"   60

CONTENTS

4. When Americans Fear Losing Their Jobs 65

"Fight Violence with Violence!" 67
Riots of the Great Depression 70
The Struggle to Organize Unions 72
The Company Guards Riot at Republic Steel 74

5. When Police Turn Violent 79

"Kill! Kill! Kill!" 81
Police Riots against Colorado Miners 82
"The Whole World Is Watching!" 84
"A Police Riot" 87

6. When Taxes Become Oppressive 91

Sam Adams, Master Rabble-Rouser 93
"Boston Harbor a Teapot Tonight!" 95
The Whiskey Rebellion 96
Farmer Riots 99

7. When Americans Clash over War 103

"No Draft! No Draft!" 104
"As Hounds Would Chase a Fox" 107
Attacks against Protesters 109
"No Military on Campus!" 110
Universities Protest the Kent State Murders 112
"Get the Traitors!" 113

8. When Despair Breeds Violence 117

After the Civil War 118
Veterans March on Washington 120

The President Wants Them Out 122
President Hoover Orders the Army to Attack 125
The Army Drives the Veterans Out 127
The Newark Six-Day Riot 130
Detroit: "It Looked Like the City Had Been Bombed" 131
"Why Is There a Violence of Despair?" 132
"Were We Becoming Conditioned to Violence?" 133
Student Riots 135
The Weathermen: "Days of Rage" 138

9. Other Causes of Riots 141

Two Thousand Lynchings 142
Mobs in the White House 143
Rumors and Mobs 144
"Martian Invaders" 144
Rock Concerts and Mob Violence 146
Sports Events and Mob Violence 147
Mob Violence and the Movies 149
Election Riots 150

10. What Does Mob Violence Accomplish? 153

Scapegoats 154
When Promises to Groups Are Broken 156

Bibliography and Recommended Reading 159

Index 165

Rage in the Streets

Introduction

What is the difference between a crowd and a mob? "To be a mob," explains language specialist Bergen Evans, "the crowd must be excited, disorderly and dangerous." And when a mob resorts to violence, the result is a riot.

There is a difference between mob action and an organized protest. An organized protest is a legitimate exercise of our First Amendment rights to express ourselves and "peaceably to assemble and to petition the Government for a redress of grievances." Mob action implies undisciplined, often violent, and usually illegal brawling to protest a grievance.

Even peaceful protest may turn into a riot. One or more rabble-rousers may incite the protesters to violence by passionate speeches, inflaming their anger to an explosive pitch. Or if police, troops, or hired thugs use violence to break up a peaceful demonstration, the demonstrators may respond in kind.

Riots often occur as tactics of last resort, when people with grievances find all other opportunities for the remedy of their afflictions blocked.

Most riots are spontaneous. They are touched off the way a

dropped match ignites tinder into a burst of flame. The spark is invariably a provocative incident or rumor. But the tinder is an accumulation of grievances by one group of the population against another group, or against the whole society.

This book also discusses vigilantes—people impatient with law enforcement's lack of efficiency or speed in dealing with alleged crimes or offenses. Vigilantes organize themselves into illegal lynch mobs and pursue the suspects. When suspects are captured, they are usually hanged or shot without a legal trial.

Mob riots should not be confused with revolutionary uprisings. Revolution seeks to overthrow a government, not just to protest injustice. A revolution may develop when a group's grievances have been ignored over a long period of time. Sometimes revolutionaries may wait until popular discontent provokes a spontaneous riot. Then they attempt to pump up the violence into a full-scale revolution.

Most Americans deplore riots as unwelcome disturbances of the peace. Yet violent protest is actually an American "tradition," beginning with riots before, during, and after the American Revolution.

Psychologist Sheldon G. Levy studied mob violence occurring over a century and a half for the Kerner Commission. President Lyndon B. Johnson appointed this commission in 1967 after widespread riots upset the nation during the 1960s. Levy found "violence throughout American history. . . . Racial violence has been consistently high for the 150-year period. . . . The problem of violence in America is not new. By its very persistence it is a more serious problem for our society than it would be were it new, for its roots run very deep."

A riot is usually a grave symptom of something desperately wrong that needs to be quickly examined and remedied. Some rioters may be inspired by an idealistic struggle against oppression, like the mobs that eventually brought on the American Revolution. In fact, much of the street violence in our history represents protest against perceived unfairness—unjust laws, abuses of power, unfair court rulings, unpopular government decisions, and the perceived inequality of the draft, slavery, and burdensome taxes.

Sadly, the largest number of riots in America yesterday and today have had their roots in racism and ethnic prejudice. This is often true even when a riot seems to be about other issues. In many cases riots have sprung from serious underlying grievances sparked into violence by immediate provocations.

MOBS DRIVEN BY PASSION

Basically, a mob is composed of a mass of individuals united by passions that drive them to disorderly conduct. To vent their rage, they threaten and attack people and property. Rioters are often people dissatisfied with some aspect of their personal lives. They may take out their frustrations on ethnic minorities or other disliked groups. Dishonest individuals often take advantage of the opportunity to indulge in looting stores for personal gain.

Our law-enforcement agencies are charged with maintaining law and order. Well-trained police and militia members know how to do this with a minimum of violence. But on many occasions they themselves have rioted out of control when subduing a crowd or mob. Victims of police brutality often fight back with riots of their own.

We sometimes think of rioting mobs as a fringe group of trouble-makers, derelicts, juvenile delinquents, and criminal types.

But Professor Richard Maxwell Brown, a historian at the College of William and Mary in Williamsburg, Virginia, points out, "We must realize that violence has not been the action only of the roughnecks and racists among us, but has been the tactic of the most upright and respected of our people. . . . We have resorted so often to violence that we have long since become a 'trigger-happy' people."

The Kerner Report declared, "One beneficent side effect of our current turmoil may be to force a harder and more candid look at our past." When we do, observed former U.S. Attorney General Ramsey Clark, we will find that "few decades in our history are unscarred by riots." In just one five-year period, from 1963 to 1968, mob disorders in the United States killed over two hundred people and seriously injured over nine thousand more. This was the stormiest period in domestic American history, except for the time of the American Revolution.

The belief that rioting mobs involve only riffraff comforts many Americans who believe all that is needed to repress the rioters is adequate force. That belief lets us ignore the serious flaws in our society that cause riots. Many people prefer not to deal with the uncomfortable changes that might be necessary to prevent such riots from recurring.

THE PSYCHOLOGY OF MOBS

Certain circumstances regularly seem to turn a crowd into a rioting mob. Most urban riots have begun between 7:00 P.M. and 12:30 A.M. on hot summer weekend nights when many people are in the streets.

The crowd must be large enough, as a rule, that those involved can be assured of anonymity. A Stanford University study indicates that people are twice as likely to resort to aggressive behavior when they are part of a group as when they are alone.

Social psychologists John Darley and Bibb Latané have found that in most street crises, each bystander looks to the others for silent guidance before acting. "One person's violent reaction at the scene of a crime," they report, "may spread, through 'contagion,' to other members of the group."

A few highly emotional people shouting out bitter grievances can whip a crowd into a frenzy.

Mobs are most likely to take matters into their own hands when a group finds that its protest against injustice is useless because "nobody's listening" or when members of the group consider their leaders either too ineffective or too meek to command attention.

Whether a crowd turns into a mob also often depends on how law-enforcement agencies behave. If the police use control measures out of proportion to the disturbance, they may provoke a crowd into rioting. Crowds often become violent when individuals are beaten or shot instead of being arrested nonviolently. This is especially true if demonstrators are protesting laws they consider unjust.

Law-enforcement agents may also be responsible for riots if they practice excessive restraint, for example, when they make no effort to stop one group from attacking another, or do so only after deliberate delay. Unwarranted delay in restoring order can quickly magnify a street brawl into a full-scale riot.

"THE COST OF NEGLECT OF THE LAST TWENTY-FIVE YEARS"

In the early 1990s there seemed to be widespread recognition that the United States was becoming a more violent society. Many people, feeling unsafe in their homes and neighborhoods, began buying guns in record numbers. Violent crime was on the rise in many cities. There was also increasing fear of racial or ethnic disorders that might trigger wild riots and cost many lives and millions of dollars in property damage.

In 1992 Senator Bill Bradley of New Jersey observed that minorities were consistently shut out of mainstream American life. "There is a kind of avoidance going on here," he declared, "avoidance of the cost of neglect of the last twenty-five years."

That same year New York Senator Daniel Patrick Moynihan observed, "We're dealing with what is now a seriously dysfunctional sector of the population. We're dealing with a population of damaged people, and no one has learned anything about undoing the damage."

There are no simple answers to these problems. An impoverished, despairing underclass will always be a major cause of violent street eruptions.

It is never enough simply to punish rioters. We also need to examine the basic reasons that compel them to riot. When we do, we will understand what needs to be done in order to prevent riots in the future.

When Court Decisions Trigger Violence

We were told a lot about the rights we were fighting for," Captain Daniel Shays thundered at a huge rally of veterans, most of them farmers. "Well, the war's over, and where are those rights? Our people are being drummed into court and jailed. Our farms are seized. We petitioned for relief, but the State Legislature is deaf. All right, I say we make our *own* laws! March with me into the towns and we'll close all the courts. If they can't try us farmers for debt, they can't send any more of us to jail! Well, are you with me?"

Twelve hundred Massachusetts veterans responded with a deafening roar of approval. They sped home to gather whatever weapons they had—rifles, knives, swords, and clubs.

Shays led them from the countryside into Northampton to attack the courthouse. The rioters seized the judge, lawyers, and court attendants and threw them into the street. They broke open the jail and freed its prisoners. Then they padlocked the courthouse.

With shouts of triumph, they stormed ahead to other towns, where they shut down and burned courthouses. Government officials tried to stop the mob but were beaten and thrown aside.

These riots occurred ten years after the victorious American army disbanded following the Revolutionary War. Most of the veterans had returned home to unplowed land and mounting debts. They were shocked to find that the country they had fought for was now firmly in the grip of wealthy war profiteers who had foreclosed on farms and homes, taking even clothing, household goods, and tools. Severe inflation and taxation in the postwar recession made the paper money in the veterans' pockets almost worthless. Flour now cost an incredible sixteen hundred dollars a barrel.

Corrupt state legislatures imposed heavy taxes upon the veterans. These went to pay off wartime obligations to the wealthy bondholders who had financed the war. Farmers who could not pay their taxes saw their homes and land seized by the state. They were also thrown in jail. When they were released, the courts ordered them to "work off" any taxes they still owed.

The veterans pleaded with the courts to suspend these harsh judgments. Their appeals fell on deaf ears.

"Is *this* what we fought for?" Shays demanded. "By God, we would be better off if we'd lost the war!"

Protest meetings all over Massachusetts demanded relief for debtors (those who owed taxes and mortgage payments). But wealthy merchants dominated the conservative state legislature. They insisted that "a bargain's a bargain, and must be made good"—the bargain being home and farm loans to the bankrupt veterans. And the courts continued to decide all debtor cases in favor of wealthy creditors.

That was why the outraged farmers rallied behind popular Daniel Shays. Shays was so penniless himself that in order to buy food for his family he was forced to sell a magnificent sword presented to him by General Lafayette for bravery in action.

Shays began his mob raids on the offending courts in 1786 and continued them through 1787. The riots shook the leaders of the new American republic. Peyton Randolph, president of the Continental Congress, was so frightened that he wrote secretly to Prince Henry

WHEN COURT DECISIONS TRIGGER VIOLENCE

of Prussia, offering to make him king of the United States if he would send troops to repress the riots. Henry ignored the offer.

From Mount Vernon, General George Washington wrote his former aide-de-camp, Colonel David Humphreys, "For God's sake, tell me, what is the cause of these commotions? If they have real grievances, redress them if possible. If they have not, employ the force of government against them at once."

Humphreys's reply denounced Shays and his mob. He wrote to Washington accusing the rioters of insisting that since they had fought to keep Britain from confiscating their own property, that property now belonged to all American veterans. He added indignantly that the Shays mob had shocked "every man of principle and property in New England!"

That was enough for Washington. He urged swift suppression of the riots for fear that the Shays Rebellion might spread to every state where there was discontent.

"A LITTLE REBELLION NOW AND THEN"

Thomas Jefferson, then American minister to France, thoroughly disagreed with suppressing the riots. "I hold that a little rebellion now and then is a good thing," he declared. "The tree of liberty must be refreshed from time to time with the blood of patriots and tyrants. It is its natural manure."

But the alarmed Congress authorized General Knox to raise a military force to confront the rioting veterans. Governor James Bowdoin of Massachusetts ordered state militia under General William Shepherd to disperse the Shays mob and arrest the ringleaders. Shays responded by leading his 1,200-man force to Springfield. They planned to attack an arsenal and seize arms.

General Shepherd and his militia stood before the arsenal waiting for them. The militiamen fired two warning volleys over the heads of the approaching mob.

Shays and his men took the overshot as a signal they would be offered only token resistance. After all, weren't many of the militiamen also veterans like themselves?

Yelling and laughing, the confident members of the mob charged straight ahead. The militiamen lowered their sights. Opening fire again, they killed three of Shays's men and wounded one.

"Murder!" screamed the rioters. "*Murder!*" Shocked and dismayed, they fled into the hills.

Governor Bowdoin and the Massachusetts legislature called out 4,400 troops to pursue the rioters. The soldiers soon reduced the scattered mob to resisting only with pitchforks and staves. Shays fled to Vermont.

The troops captured 150 rioters. The courts tried many of them and 14 were sentenced to death by hanging.

But statewide sympathy for the Shays Rebellion caused popular indignation. In the next election, voters swept Governor Bowdoin and the legislature out of office. Some members of Shays's mob even won seats in the new legislature. They lost no time in shaping new laws to give relief to poor farmers.

The death sentences were not carried out. The imprisoned rioters were either pardoned promptly or given brief jail terms. Finally, in 1788, the legislature passed a general amnesty, permitting Shays to return home to Massachusetts.

The desperation of this riot, it turned out, had shocked Americans into realizing that something was seriously wrong with their laws.

"These disorders are evident marks of a defective government," Washington wrote Marquis de Lafayette on March 25, 1787. "Indeed the thinking people of this country are now so well satisfied of this fact that most of the legislatures have appointed . . . delegates to meet at Philadelphia . . . to revise and correct the defects of the Federal system."

The role of riot leaders is often overestimated, although they frequently do play a significant part in mob action. Sometimes individuals with political ambitions may make inflammatory speeches to attract attention to themselves and win a following. But the direct cause of the Shays riots was the anger of farmers over unfair court decisions. Had there been no widespread indignation over the courts' verdicts, no agitator could have spurred rioters to shut the courts down.

In 1786 the new American government had failed to make fair provisions for veterans to return safely to the farm life they had left to fight in the War of Independence. Public recognition of this injustice helped bring about the Constitutional Convention and the Eighth Amendment to the Constitution, which prohibits excessive bail or fines and cruel or unusual punishment.

"GET A ROPE! LYNCH HER!"

White citizens of Little Rock, Arkansas, were stunned and disbelieving. The district court had ordered the school board of Little Rock to admit black children to all-white Central High School, enforcing a three-year-old Supreme Court decision. In *Brown v. Board of Education* (1954), the court had ruled that "separate but equal" schools for black and white children were unconstitutional. The court had ordered all schools to integrate their classes.

In Little Rock the superintendent of schools and the school board reluctantly complied with the district court order. They scheduled nine African-American children to enter Central High School, which had over two thousand white students.

In August 1957 Arkansas segregationists demanded that Governor Orval Faubus block the admission of the nine black students to Central High. On September 2, one day before school was to begin, Faubus dispatched National Guard units to the school grounds. He declared the school off-limits to black students, on the pretext of "preserving the peace."

It was the first time since the Civil War that a governor had openly challenged federal law by the use of state troops.

For three weeks the guardsmen prevented the African-American students from entering Central High. Finally the District Court of Arkansas ruled that Governor Faubus's action was illegal. It compelled the withdrawal of the guardsmen and ordered Little Rock police to protect the black children as they entered the high school on September 23. Faubus grimly predicted that mob violence would erupt.

Earlier that month a furious mob of nearly a thousand white citizens had gathered outside the school, determined to defy the district court order and keep the black students out. Many of the mob were armed with baseball bats and rocks. They screamed insults and threats at the frightened black youngsters brought to Central High.

When Elizabeth Eckford, 15, tried to pass the blockade, she was forced to retreat. A horde of white women pursued her, shrieking, "Get a rope! Lynch her!" Benjamin Fine, education editor of the *New York Times*, who had come to Little Rock to witness the event, put his arm around the trembling girl to protect her. The weeping Elizabeth was hurried to safety aboard a passing bus. The frustrated mob turned on Fine. Instead of coming to his defense, Little Rock police threatened to arrest him for "inciting to riot."

On September 23, a mob of a thousand gathered as the nine black children managed to enter the school under police escort. White students pushed, shoved, insulted, and threatened them. Meanwhile the mob outside began hurling rocks and surging through police lines. The violence forced the principal to send the black children home for their own safety.

Next day Mayor Woodrow Mann wired the White House: "The immediate need for federal troops is urgent. The mob is much larger in numbers at 8:00 A.M. than at any time yesterday. People are converging on the scene from all directions and engaging in fisticuffs and other acts of violence. Situation is out of control and police cannot disperse the mob."

President Dwight D. Eisenhower was outraged by the mob's defiance of the orders of both the Supreme Court and the Arkansas District Court. On September 24 he rushed a thousand army paratroopers to Little Rock. He angrily issued a proclamation to "command all persons engaged in such obstruction of justice to cease and desist therefrom and to disperse forthwith. . . . The federal law . . . cannot be flouted with impunity by any individual or any mob of extremists."

The African-American children returned to school behind federal bayonets. To protect them from hostile white students, the troops had to escort them to and from classrooms. They also had to protect them from the frenzied mob as they came to and left school.

The president kept the paratroopers in Little Rock until October 1, when he replaced them with federalized national guardsmen. The guardsmen were charged with protecting the black students at Central High for the balance of the school year.

In 1958 Governor Faubus closed Little Rock's four high schools, rather than open them on an integrated basis. That year he sought to turn them into private, segregated academies. But the Supreme Court ruled against this attempt to evade the law. The white citizens of Little Rock were finally compelled to accept integration of their schools.

Instead of enforcing segregation, the rioters' actions had had the opposite effect. Their disorders were an important factor in causing Congress to pass the Civil Rights Act of 1957, the first civil rights measure to pass in eighty-two years. Among its provisions was enforcement of court orders desegregating all public schools.

At the same time the Little Rock riots caused Senate Democrats to worry about losing southern white votes. So they watered down the Civil Rights Act to eliminate all provisions except those relating to voting rights.

SCHOOL BUSES DYNAMITED

Twenty-four years later the North experienced a violent reaction against court-ordered integration. In September 1971 black children and their parents were nervous and excited as school was about to open in Pontiac, Michigan. The Federal District Court had ordered the city to bus eighty-seven hundred black children to all-white schools outside their neighborhoods. Northern segregation had been maintained until then by practices that prevented African-Americans from moving into white neighborhoods.

A dynamite blast suddenly erupted at the Pontiac school bus depot. It set fire to and destroyed ten school buses.

White racists vowed that they would never allow black children to be bused to all-white public schools, no matter what the district court decreed. On Labor Day thousands of white parents and children staged a huge protest demonstration through downtown Pontiac, shouting threatening slogans.

Next day school buses set out to pick up children in the ghetto areas. Nine furious white mothers dashed out of a mob and chained themselves to the gates of the bus yard. They formed a human barrier to prevent the buses from leaving. Police cut the chains and arrested the screaming women.

The buses rolled. A mob of bitter white parents and children blocked school entrances as the buses arrived. They shrieked insults and threats at the black children, punching them as police hurried them through the mob. Inside the classrooms hardly a white student was to be seen. Many white parents were boycotting the schools. The boycott held solid for two days.

More mobs rioted in front of the schools. Gradually, however, anger about the court decision was overshadowed by parental fears that their children would fall behind in their studies. White students began straggling back to classes. Soon attendance had returned to normal.

WHEN COURT DECISIONS TRIGGER VIOLENCE

THE RODNEY KING CASE

Siren wailing, a police car pursued a speeding Hyundai along a Los Angeles freeway on March 3, 1991. The police finally forced the car to stop. Four white officers surrounded it with guns drawn, and they ordered three African-Americans out of the car.

They forced the suspects to lie facedown on the ground. Two of the passengers submitted to handcuffs. But the driver, 25-year-old Rodney King, sought to struggle up to his knees. The police pushed him down. He made it back to his feet and lunged angrily at one officer. The police fired two Taser stun darts at him. Each carried thirty thousand volts of electricity.

King slipped to the ground, helpless. The police then clubbed him viciously over fifty times, for fully eighty-one seconds. They also stomped on his prostrate body and kicked him savagely seven times.

Other white officers arrived on the scene. They simply watched while the other policemen broke King's skull in nine places with their batons.

All the police were unaware that they were being watched by George Holliday, a plumber, from his apartment window. He filmed King's beating with a camcorder. Subsequently he released the video-tape to TV studios. It became one of the most widely watched news clips in the history of TV. Stations across the country showed it over and over. Millions of viewers were outraged.

"Except for the fortuitous presence of a camera," declared American Civil Liberties Union (ACLU) Executive Director Ira Glasser, "we might never have known about this incident. . . . Charges would have been made, the accused officers would have denied the charges, and [Los Angeles Police] Chief Gates would have backed them up. . . . The incident would have been forgotten and gone unremedied."

But now thousands of indignant Los Angeles citizens demanded the firing of Chief Daryl Gates for tolerating police brutality in the LAPD. Public uproar compelled a trial of the four policemen on charges of assault and falsifying police reports about the King incident. The officers' defense counsel protested that they could not get a fair trial in Los Angeles. A judge transferred the case to nearby Simi Valley, a white, middle-class suburb.

The jurors selected to hear the case included ten whites, one Latino, and one Asian—but no African-Americans.

On April 29, 1992, a crowd of blacks gathered outside the courthouse as the jury deliberated. They roared, "Guilty! Guilty! Guilty!" That verdict seemed inevitable, since the jury had been shown the videotape of King's brutal beating.

Incredibly, the nervous jury returned a verdict of "not guilty" for three of the policemen, and the jurors declared a mistrial for the fourth. The news shocked the crowd outside and astounded the nation. A *Newsweek* survey showed that 73 percent of white Americans and 92 percent of African-Americans considered the verdict a total miscarriage of justice.

The court's verdict touched off a tremendous riot in a largely black Los Angeles district called Watts. Angry mobs of African-Americans ran through the streets in a wild rampage. They were joined by Central American Latino gangs. The rioters torched the guardhouse outside police headquarters, set the Los Angeles city hall on fire, and trashed the criminal court building.

"THE CITY WENT WILD"

Store after store went up in flames. Smoke engulfed the neighborhood. It was so thick that most of Los Angeles International Airport had to be shut down for a time. Firefighters with police escorts tried to extinguish some 1,000 conflagrations. But by 10:00 P.M. on the day of the verdict the rioters had set twenty-five square blocks of central Los Angeles ablaze. Their torches and firebombs reduced stores, gas stations, buildings, and supermarkets to ashes.

Gang members hurled stones and bottles at passing cars, breaking windows, as more and more people rushed to join the raging mobs. They dragged white motorists from cars and assaulted them. Rioters set cars afire.

TV news cameras filmed rioters dragging Reginald Oliver Denny, 36, a white truck driver, out of his cab. They kicked him and smashed him on the head with a large brick. A black aerospace engineer and three other African-American onlookers saved Denny's life by rushing to his rescue and driving him to a hospital.

Dramatic TV and radio broadcasts of the riot brought more Los Angeles street gangs swarming to the scene, brandishing pipes, sticks, and baseball bats. Police said most of the people who attacked whites and set fires were blacks and Latinos with criminal records. Taking advantage of the riot, the gangs led a looting spree. Poor Latinos, blacks, Asians, and whites joined in.

The mob smashed store windows and raced off with grocery cartons, cases of beer, stereos, computers, and sports equipment. Gang members also looted seventeen hundred weapons from gun stores and pawnshops. They began firing some wildly, killing a white motorcyclist and driver. Police stayed largely absent from the riot for some five hours. When they finally arrived, they killed some African-Americans and Latinos in shootouts.

"With the Watts riots in 1965 it built and built and on the third day the city went mad," observed Police Commander Robert Gil. "This was completely different—the city went wild in just an hour and a half."

Korean merchants in Watts suffered some of the worst damage. They watched over a hundred of their stores go up in flames.

Charles Kim wept as he saw his store burn down. "This is not America!" he cried. "We are all brothers. Why are they doing this?"

"The situation," Chief Gates admitted bleakly, "is not under control." On the second day California Governor Pete Wilson, Los Angeles Mayor Tom Bradley, and Chief Gates imposed a dawn-to-dusk curfew. President Bush declared the city a disaster area. He sent army troops and 1,000 federal officers to suppress the riot. Wilson dispatched 2,000 national guardsmen and 750 highway patrolmen.

Riots persisted into the third day. Rodney King made a tearful appeal to TV cameras. "We've got to quit," he quavered. "We got to quit. Can't we all get along?"

Los Angeles was not the only city to suffer because of the Simi Valley jury verdict. Riots erupted in San Francisco, Seattle, Atlanta, and New York City.

The eighty-one seconds of videotape that showed the police beating Rodney King had resulted in a "not guilty" verdict that provoked three days of savage rioting. The violence, which erupted in other parts of the city as well, had killed 45 people, injured almost 2,400, sent 9,500 to jail, set 623 fires, and caused property damage estimated at over a billion dollars. Watts was reduced to shambles. Between 25,000 and 40,000 people were thrown out of work. Poor Watts residents were unable to buy food, cash checks, or get gas for their cars in their own neighborhood.

Police Chief Gates was blamed for tolerating police brutality and for his delay in getting police to curb the rioters. The Reverend Jesse Jackson led a protest march of two thousand people to LAPD headquarters, shouting, "Daryl Gates must go!" Gates balked at resigning for weeks, but finally, on June 26, 1992, he yielded reluctantly to public demands for his resignation.

Analysts attributed LAPD police brutality to poor training, racism, slack departmental discipline, and the tradition of covering up for cops who used undue violence.

No one disputed that the flash point that had set off the riot was the "not guilty" verdict reached by the Simi Valley jury. But most commentators agreed that the black community's underlying grievances were the fuel that fed the riots.

"WE ARE SITTING ON A POWDER KEG"

Los Angeles Councilman Michael Woo warned, "I don't want to pre-dict another round of violence, but one thing that is clear from the last time is that it doesn't take much to set off violence. We are sitting on a powder keg in this city."

(Watts had exploded in a major riot once before, in 1965, sparked by rumors that police had beaten a black motorist for a traffic vio-lation and had clubbed down a pregnant black woman who protested. The riot had raged for six days, involving ten thousand people. Thirty-five had been killed and nine hundred injured; some two hundred buildings had been burned down.

The underlying cause of black rage in 1965 had been decades of neglect of the needs of the residents of inner cities. The blacks of Watts had felt victimized by lack of jobs and by rundown schools, exorbitant ghetto prices, lack of low-cost housing, and police bru-tality. Twenty-seven years later little had changed—and much of the damage caused in 1965 was still unrepaired.)

Sociologists viewed the 1992 Watts riot as a "final wake-up call" to the nation. It shocked all America into a renewed recognition of the grievances smoldering in the ghettos.

In a survey of a thousand people who either worked or lived in Los Angeles, three out of four blamed the 1992 riot on racial tensions caused by police brutality. Three out of five also blamed the poor economic conditions in Watts, where 30 percent of blacks were with-out jobs.

There were other contributory causes. Unemployment had wors-ened the breakdown of family units in Watts. It had also caused a number of jobless blacks, especially youths, to turn in desperation to dealing drugs. That had led to further clashes with the police.

A Los Angeles housing study made after the riots also blamed the shortage of affordable housing for African-Americans. Frustration ran high because 75 percent of poor families had to pay over half their income for rent. One in four ghetto families was forced to live in overcrowded, rundown slum apartments.

Blacks also strongly resented the large influx of Latinos and Asians into their neighborhoods. "What they see are people who are not black," observed sociologist Ivan Light of the University of California at Los Angeles, "who are soaking up economic opportunities that ought to be available to them. They see people who are taking their money out of their neighborhood."

Korean-owned stores became special targets of both black and Latino rioters. "This wasn't a race riot," suggested sociologist Joel Kotkin. "It was a class riot." It expressed the resentment of a new generation of left-out, alienated ghetto youths.

Because of the looting, rioters lost a lot of sympathy for their protest against court injustice. "As the rioting goes on and the looters come out of stores," observed University of Chicago sociologist William Julius Wilson, "people shift their anger toward the rioters."

Despite this, the 1992 Watts riot did succeed in focusing attention once more on the depressed conditions in the ghetto. A *U.S. News and World Report* poll found that 63 percent of Americans were now willing to pay higher taxes to provide more government aid for inner-city minorities. Governor Wilson signed into law a package of measures to provide almost three hundred million dollars in government spending and tax credits to benefit the riot-damaged areas.

The riot also brought a new police chief, Willie Williams, to Los Angeles. He pledged to train officers of the LAPD to have greater sensitivity in dealing with the city's nonwhite population.

And although the Simi Valley jury had acquitted the police in the Rodney King affair, a federal grand jury indicted them on a charge of violating his civil rights. At the second trial, lasting six weeks, the police argued that King had looked dangerous and had fought back, but other footage from the Holliday film failed to show this. Melanie Singer, a police officer who had witnessed the affair, also contradicted her fellow officers' version of what had happened, supporting King's story.

As the jury deliberated for six days, Los Angeles prepared to face another terrible riot if the police were found innocent again. But this time, on August 4, 1993, only two officers were acquitted, while the sergeant in charge and the officer who had beaten King most severely were found guilty. Los Angeles minorities hailed the verdict and the city remained peaceful. The convicted officers received minimal sentences of thirty months each.

Mob riots often break out when courts render a decision that seems shockingly unjust to the minority group affected by it. A *Newsweek* survey asked: "Compared to whites charged with crimes, are black people charged with crimes treated more harshly . . . in this country's justice system?" Only 46 percent of whites indicated that is the case, but 75 percent of African-Americans said yes.

OPERATION RESCUE

Moral outrage sparked tumultuous demonstrations in 1991 by anti-abortion activists. In Brookline, Massachusetts, and Binghamton, New York, anti-abortionists organized themselves as "Operation Rescue," in protest against the 1973 Supreme Court decision *Roe v. Wade*, which had declared abortion legal.

To block women from entering clinics where legal abortions were performed, the protesters lay down or sat three rows deep in the street outside the clinics. Police had to carry them off physically. In 1991 Operation Rescue also blockaded clinics in Wichita, Kansas. The resulting uproar led to over two thousand arrests and a police cost to the city of over half a million dollars.

The Operation Rescue mobs were convinced that every fetus has a right to be born, thus making abortion "baby murder." Moral outrage also inflamed "pro-choice" activists, who argued that a fetus is not a developed baby and that a woman has the right to choose to terminate a pregnancy without having the government tell her what she might or might not do with her own body.

Operation Rescue demonstrators hoped they would be able to shut down abortion clinics and arouse popular support for outlawing the right of women to terminate an unwanted pregnancy. But they lost much public support in 1993 when, in front of a Pensacola, Florida, clinic, one of their demonstrators shot and killed Dr. David Gunn, who performed abortions. Even many groups opposing abortion condemned Operation Rescue's tactics. But the bad publicity that year did not prevent Operation Rescue from staging picket lines in front of the homes of doctors who performed abortions in an attempt to intimidate them.

T W O

When Intolerance
Leads to Violence

The rumor flashed all over Boston. A Catholic nun, Sister Mary John, was reported to have incurred the displeasure of a tyrannical mother superior at the Ursuline convent in the Charlestown area. Sister Mary John was rumored to be imprisoned in the convent's "dungeons," which (some people claimed) overflowed with insubordinate nuns and children imprisoned to do penance. Upon escaping she allegedly had been captured and dragged back to the underground cells.

This rumor outraged thousands of Boston Protestants who considered Catholics "un-American," tools of a Vatican plot to take over the United States. Widely circulated books had already spread gruesome tales about "works of the devil" that went on in convent dungeons. Nuns were supposedly held as "white slaves" for priests. Many non-Catholics believed these libels and swallowed the rumor about Sister Mary John.

Posters suddenly appeared all over Charlestown: TO THE SELECTMEN OF CHARLESTOWN! GENTLEMEN, IT IS YOUR DUTY TO HAVE THIS AFFAIR INVESTIGATED IMMEDIATELY. IF NOT, THE TRUCKMEN OF BOSTON WILL DEMOLISH THE NUNNERY THURSDAY NIGHT!

A committee of five Charlestown selectmen hastily visited the

Ursuline convent to probe the allegation. The indignant mother superior, Mother Saint George, produced Sister Mary John, who assured the visitors that she was not being held a captive. Later she also offered to show one selectman through the empty basement of the convent—the alleged dungeon—but when Mother Saint George insisted he go alone, he fled.

By the time the selectmen reported that their investigation found no truth to the rumor, anti-Catholic extremists had already fanned mob hysteria to fever pitch. Bostonians were eager to believe the worst.

It was August 11, 1834. At nine o'clock that night a furious Boston mob of thousands rushed upon the Ursuline convent. They howled, "Free the prisoners!" The uproar wakened children asleep in the dormitory of the convent's boarding school.

"DOWN WITH THE CONVENT!"

Louisa Goddard, one of those schoolgirls, recalled later, "I heard—what shall I call it?—a shout, a cry, a howl, a yell? It was the sound of the mob, a voice of the night, indeed, that made [the night] hideous. . . . The mob gave one roar as it crossed Charlestown Bridge, and then observed profound silence till it reached the convent grounds. My heart beat thick and fast. . . .

"A horrible yell suddenly rent the air within a few yards of the window at which I was standing, and a host of dark figures rushed into view. . . . I flew across the room to Elizabeth Williams's bed, shaking her and crying out, 'Wake up, wake up, the mob has really come!' She started up screaming. . . . All the girls in the dormitory suddenly wakened, scream[ing] in concert . . . , 'Oh, the mob, the mob—we shall all be killed!'"

Nuns rushed to soothe the children. But they were frightened themselves as cries of the mob filled the night—"Down with the convent! . . . Free the hidden nun! . . . Release all the prisoners in the dungeon!" Mob leaders began pounding on the convent door, demanding admittance.

A defiant Mother Saint George opened the door and confronted the mob. She declared icily that the selectmen had already investigated the rumors and declared them false. The rioters demanded that she step aside and let them search for themselves.

"Disperse immediately!" she cried out angrily. "For if you don't, the Bishop has twenty thousand Irishmen at his command in Boston, and they will whip you all into the sea!"

At this, wrathful rioters began hurling stones. Mother Saint George slammed the door shut and bolted it.

Rioters lighted torches and set aflame a pile of tar barrels they had brought along. The bonfire was a signal to summon supporters from all over Charlestown. The mob quickly swelled to four thousand. They opened barrels of rum, and drunken war cries soon filled the night. Rioters smashed convent windows and tried to break down the heavy door.

Mother Saint George tried to appeal to the mob from an upstairs window. Two shots fired at her forced her to retreat to the children's dormitory. By this time the children and the nuns were in a state of utter terror. Some children had fainted.

THE CONVENT IS STORMED

Lighting more torches at midnight, the howling mob stormed the convent. Rioters burst into the building through the smashed windows. Mother Saint George hastily led the children out through a back entrance to a sheltered garden.

The rioters raced from attic to cellar in a drunken, fruitless search for a dungeon with imprisoned nuns. Frustrated, they vandalized furniture, books, and religious objects. They tossed musical instruments out windows, and they looted silverware. Throwing bedding and schoolbooks in a heap on the first floor, they lighted bonfires. Some rioters dashed through the convent with torches, setting the drapes on fire.

"Get the mother superior!" one cried. "Burn the old witch!"

Rioters ran about searching for her. Mother Saint George, the nuns, and the children huddled together in the garden in terrified silence. Then, under cover of darkness, a rescuer tore some palings off the fence enclosure and helped them escape. Three children later died from the effects of exposure and shock.

The spectacular blaze set by the rioters brought eleven fire companies from Boston, suburban Charlestown, and Cambridge. They could not put out the conflagration, however, because the mob cut their fire hoses. Rioters threatened to assault any firefighter who attempted to save the convent.

At dawn the convent was in smoking ruins, and the rum barrels were empty. The rioters left, cheering and singing.

They returned the next night to destroy fences, trees, and anything else still standing on the convent site. Next day another rumor circulated that Bishop Fenwick of Boston had called upon the city's Irish workers to avenge the outrage. That night a mob of a thousand Protestants armed with knives and pistols formed defiantly in front of the Catholic church in Charlestown.

But no Irish workers appeared to challenge them.

Although this infamous anti-Catholic riot was sparked by the false rumor about Sister Mary John, the attack on the convent was basically the result of intense religious prejudice.

"A BASE AND COWARDLY ACT"

Famine in Ireland between 1830 and 1840 sent masses of Irish Catholic workers flooding into the cities of the American Northeast. They sought jobs in the rapidly growing American industries. Protestant workers felt threatened by the willingness of the Irish to work long hours for low wages, and mobs wrecked the immigrants' homes and neighborhoods. During this period no less than thirty-five major anti-Catholic riots took place in the United States.

Protestants also felt hostile toward the Catholic churches, schools, and convents springing up in their midst. Anti-Catholic newspapers printed lurid propaganda tracts imported from abroad, bearing such titles as *Forty Popish Frauds Detected and Disclosed.*

The mob's attack on the Ursuline convent backfired against the rioters at first. Boston Mayor Theodore Lyman, Jr., called a town meeting to denounce the riot as "a base and cowardly act." An investigation led to the arrest of thirteen rioters on charges of arson, which at that time was punishable by death.

But when the defendants were tried in Concord, a mob surged on the court. Rioters hanged court officials in effigy, and they threatened to attack witnesses, the judge, and the jury if the defendants were found guilty. The cowed jury freed all the defendants but one teenager, who was soon pardoned by the governor.

The mob cheered the freed rioters as they left court and honored them with a fifty-gun salute. The Massachusetts legislature refused to pay the Ursuline convent for the damage caused by the rioters.

Mob spirit had triumphed over religious liberty in Boston. As a silent reproach, the Catholic community let the ruins of the convent stand for the next fifty years.

Religious prejudice against Catholics in the United States persisted for a long time. During the 1840s Protestant workingmen grew resentful of the progress Catholics had made in winning better jobs and gaining political clout. They organized under the name Native Americans but acquired the mocking nickname of "Know-Nothings." When questioned about their violent anti-Catholic activities, they would simply shrug and say, "I know nothing about that."

In 1854 one Know-Nothing mob in St. Louis, Missouri, attacked Catholics to drive them away from election polls. A St. Louis newspaper reported, "For forty-eight hours the city has been the scene of one of the most appalling riots that has ever taken place in the country. Men have been butchered like cattle, property destroyed, and anarchy reigns supreme. . . . The military and police have, thus far, been unable to check the onward march of lawlessness and crime. The scenes of last night were terrible, never, we hope, to be enacted again."

But they were. Again and again.

PERSECUTING THE CHINESE

A furious white mob surrounded the Chinese district in Los Angeles. Frightened Chinese barricaded themselves in their houses. The rioters stormed their homes, racing over the rooftops with axes and guns. They smashed holes in roofs and threw fireballs into the houses to drive out the occupants. The Chinese fled when their homes went up in flames, but the mobs shot people down as they appeared. Other Chinese men, women, and children were dragged out and hanged in batches from awnings and wagon tops.

Before the rampage was over, the mob had shot or lynched nineteen Chinese. Then the rioters looted all the stores in Chinatown.

The year was 1871. Similar riots persisted in the West all through the 1870s and 1880s. In 1873 one eyewitness reported, "It was a common sight in San Francisco and other cities to see Chinese pelted with stones or mud, beaten or kicked, having vegetables or laundry stolen from their baskets, and even having their queues [pigtails] cut." Mobs burned Chinese laundries, and some victims who tried to escape were forced back into the flames.

Police made little effort to stop the rioters.

In 1877 white workers in San Francisco formed a mob, shouting, "The Chinese must go!" They raided Chinatown, beating up the Chinese and burning their laundries and shops. They set fire to the docks of the Pacific Mall Steamship Company, which had brought in the immigrants, and they torched a lumberyard that employed Chinese.

Many Chinese took jobs or operated businesses no white men wanted but that were an essential part of daily life, such as operating laundries. Yet at the end of the 1870s anti-Chinese feeling exploded violently once again, this time in Denver. A white mob attacked the Chinese quarter, beating the residents and looting their homes and shops. White friends saved one Chinese man by nailing him in a box and carrying him through the raging mob.

The only white man to defend the Chinese openly was a gambler who expressed the cynical attitude of the day when he defied the rioters. With two leveled guns, he roared, "If you kill Wong, who in hell will do my laundry?"

The basic cause of rioting against the Chinese was prejudice. The Chinese were considered much too racially "different" to be assimilated into white American society. White Americans also viewed the low standard of living of the Chinese immigrants as a threat to the American way of life. Once again American workers considered their jobs threatened, this time by the Chinese, who worked for low wages and were hired as strikebreakers.

Mobs could persecute the Chinese with impunity all through the 1870s and 1880s. "The hoodlums need have no fear of punishment," the *New York Times* observed in 1874. "Of course, the municipal authorities . . . nominally object to the threatened riot, but inasmuch as the Chinese have no votes, while every hoodlum polls at least a score [votes at least twenty times], no very vigorous interference with the popular will need be apprehended."

The Chinese had first immigrated to the United States to seek their fortunes in the gold rush of 1848. Their numbers and their different culture aroused antagonism among white miners.

"The manner and habits of the Chinese are very repugnant to Americans in California," observed Frank Soule in his 1854 book, *The Annals of San Francisco*. "There is a strong feeling—prejudice it may be—existing in California against all Chinamen." White mobs robbed, beat, and frequently murdered the Chinese with impunity—hence the saying "Not a Chinaman's chance." The term *Chinaman* is considered derogatory today.

In 1863 another huge wave of Chinese immigrants arrived in the United States. This time they were recruited by the Central Pacific Railroad to do dangerous, exhausting pick-and-shovel and dynamite work, building the line connecting the Union Pacific.

When the job was finished, the Chinese returned to the West Coast to look for new work. White construction workers attacked them shouting, "Go home, John!" (The Chinese were often referred to slightingly as "John Chinaman.")

BARRING CHINESE IMMIGRATION

Labor riots often reflected the determination of white workers to keep ethnic groups out of their unions, factories, and communities. This applied especially to the Chinese. The anti-Chinese riots led to the formation of the Workingmen's party in 1877, dedicated to expelling and excluding the Chinese from the United States. Its views and goals were shared by future U.S. President James A. Garfield, who, as a Congressman in 1877, believed that while Indians and blacks could be assimilated culturally, "not so in the least degree with the Chinaman."

In 1879 riots and agitation by the Workingmen's party led Congress to introduce legislation excluding Chinese immigrants from the United States. Then-president Rutherford B. Hayes declared, "I am satisfied the present Chinese labor invasion . . . is pernicious and should be discouraged."

California did not wait for national legislation to be implemented. In the spring of 1879 the state legislature already forbade employment of Chinese by corporations and ordered the punishment of any company importing them. On election day, out of 155,000 votes cast, only 883 Californians favored allowing Chinese immigration to continue.

President Hayes yielded to railroad and corporate executives who wanted to assure themselves of a steady supply of cheap labor and demanded that he veto the federal exclusion bill. Still, Hayes tried to persuade the Chinese government to restrict immigration to the United States voluntarily. He was unsuccessful.

This attempt did not satisfy the Workingmen's party. Party members raised the specter of four hundred million Chinese "invading" the United States, "conquering" it by sheer numbers, unless strict immigration barriers were raised. In 1882 Congress passed another bill calling for absolute exclusion of Chinese laborers for at least ten years. President Chester Arthur signed the Exclusion Act into law.

This was the first time people wishing to come to the United States were denied the opportunity because of their race. That prejudicial policy lasted, through constant renewals of the Exclusion Act, for half a century.

Many American Westerners, not satisfied with the Exclusion Act, demanded the expulsion of Chinese already here. In September 1885 a mob of striking white miners in Rock Springs, Wyoming, attacked 150 workers from China who had replaced them in the mines. Driving all the Chinese out of town, the union rioters killed twenty-eight, wounded fifteen, and burned their dwellings to the ground. The arrival of federal troops rushed to Rock Springs by President Grover Cleveland saved the lives of many of the Chinese who had fled. A local grand jury refused to indict any of the white miners.

This riot inspired similar anti-Chinese activity throughout the West. In Tacoma, Washington, mobs attacked the Chinese district. They forced all Chinese, at gunpoint, onto wagons and a train for deportation.

A mob in Seattle, Washington, rounded up 350 Chinese, drove them to the city's docks in wagons, and forced them aboard a steamer bound for China. Some immigrants who could not be squeezed aboard now voluntarily sought to return home. Gun battles broke out between the mob and a Home Guard sent to protect the Chinese. President Cleveland had to declare martial law. It was not lifted until the remaining Chinese had been shipped out.

"MURDERED BY A MOB"

President Cleveland noted that "in the Wyoming territory numbers of unoffending Chinamen . . . [were] murdered by a mob." He urged the protection of all Chinese, insisting that violators of their civil rights be brought to justice. He blamed race prejudice, declaring, "It exists in a large part of our domain, jeopardizing our domestic peace and the good relations we strive to maintain with China."

But Cleveland negotiated a new treaty with the Chinese ambassador in Washington, totally excluding Chinese laborers. To sugarcoat the pill, he offered to pay China an indemnity of a quarter of a million dollars for the damage caused by anti-Chinese rioting on the West Coast.

Cleveland was angered when the Chinese government refused to honor the treaty. He told the Senate, "The experiment of blending social habits and mutual race idiosyncrasies of the Chinese laboring classes with those of the great body of the people of the United States has proved by the experience of twenty years to be in every sense unwise, unpolitic, and injurious."

This view was later echoed by Theodore Roosevelt. When he ran for the White House, he declared that the presence of Chinese in the United States was "ruinous to the white race."

The anti-Chinese riots of the 1870s and the 1880s reflected the race prejudice of most Americans at that time. Through violent action they compelled the government to enact their prejudice into law.

"HANG THE JEW!"

During the nineteenth and much of the twentieth centuries, southern mobs usually directed their actions against three principal minority groups—blacks, Catholics, and Jews.

Russian persecution of Jews in the 1880s and 1890s set off a wave of Jewish immigration to the United States. Like the Catholics and Chinese, the Jews aroused a hostile reaction among Caucasian "native Americans," particularly in the deep South.

Thomas E. Watson of Georgia led the anti-Semitic bigots. From 1906 to 1913 he concentrated his attacks on Catholics and blacks in his weekly paper, the *Jeffersonian,* and his monthly *Watson's Magazine.* A former candidate for President, Watson had grown rich investing in plantations worked by sharecroppers. He was ambitious to become a senator and sought support by appealing to intolerance.

His big opportunity came in April 1913 with the arrest of Leo Frank, a Jewish graduate of Cornell—and thus a northerner—who was part-owner of a Marietta, Georgia, pencil factory. Frank was accused of abusing and strangling to death 14-year-old Mary Phagan in the factory's cellar. Before she died, however, she managed to scribble a note accusing an African-American man of the crime. Factory worker Jim Conley was arrested. But he was allowed to plea-bargain for a light sentence in return for naming Frank as the killer.

On the day of Frank's trial, an anti-Semitic editorial in Watson's paper whipped a mob into a fury. Rioters surrounded the courthouse. They threatened court officials: "Hang the Jew or we'll hang you!"

Judge and jury swiftly convicted Frank on no evidence except Conley's accusation. When the mob outside heard that Frank had been sentenced to hang, they roared approval and danced with joy in the streets. Conley was convicted only as an accessory, and he was sent to labor on a chain gang for one year.

Leading newspapers throughout the country denounced the trial as a travesty of justice. Watson lashed back in his publications, declaring Frank and all Jews "ritual murderers."

Georgia Governor John M. Slaton responded to national indignation over the case by commuting Frank's sentence to life imprisonment. Watson denounced the governor as "King of the Jews and Traitors."

Agitated by Watson's ravings, an armed mob styled themselves a "vigilance committee." They drove in cars to the prison farm where Frank was held. The warden and guards offered no resistance when the rioters seized Frank and drove off with him.

The mob hanged him.

"A Vigilance Committee redeems Georgia," Watson gloated in his weekly, "and carries out the sentence of the law."

The *Boston Traveler* spoke for a shocked North: "In this crowning demonstration of her inherent savagery, Georgia stands revealed before the world in her naked barbarian brutality."

But Watson got what he was after. He won election to the Senate in 1920. Here, as a notorious racial and religious bigot, he continued to represent prejudiced mobs of Georgia.

The mob that murdered Leo Frank, an innocent man, had not done so because they believed him guilty. He was simply a convenient target for their ignorant ethnic hatred—he was a Jew from the North. As in the attacks on the Ursuline convent in Boston and on the Chinese workers in the West, none of the mob in Georgia were ever arrested or charged with murder.

WARTIME HYSTERIA

When Woodrow Wilson declared war against Germany in 1917, he worried about the violence he was unleashing at home. "The spirit of ruthless brutality will enter the very fiber of our national life," he warned, "infecting Congress, the courts, the policeman on the beat, the man in the streets."

His prophecy was quickly fulfilled.

In an atmosphere charged with suspicion and bigotry, vigilante mobs equated any criticism of the government with disloyalty. Mobs sprang up all over the country to persecute as "un-American" all who dared challenge the necessity for World War I.

Wilson's attorney general, A. Mitchell Palmer, viewed all dissent as treason. After the Bolshevik Revolution swept Russia in 1917, Palmer launched a wholesale crackdown on aliens and citizens he suspected of being radicals, and he made mass arrests.

Vigilante mobs, encouraged by Palmer, smeared yellow paint on the houses of pacifists. They raided schools to tear up German-language textbooks, and they compelled aliens to kiss the American flag in public. They attacked radical labor meetings, especially unions with a large foreign membership, like the militant Industrial Workers of the World (IWW).

Some of the mobs were members of the American Protective League (APL). One writer called the APL "a government-sponsored lynch mob." Its members punished strikers by beatings, kidnappings, lynchings, and mass deportations out of state. Police ignored their actions.

As war hysteria soared, Congress passed the Sedition Act in May 1918, outlawing all criticism of the government, armed forces, Constitution, flag, or participation in the war. Aliens or naturalized Americans who spoke broken English were suspect, especially those who belonged to the IWW.

To unite public opinion behind the war effort, Wilson established the Committee on Public Information, headed by journalist George Creel. Its propaganda whipped up a frenzy of ultrapatriotic hatred of the "Hun" and then turned against its own people. Hysterical mobs tore down statues of famous German-Americans such as Carl Schurz, secretary of the interior under President Hayes. Immigrants who knew no English were beaten for speaking German in public, and pacifists were attacked as "dirty German spies."

Creel later admitted, "The sweep of mean intolerance, of course, developed a mob spirit. . . . The press, from which we had the right to expect help, failed us miserably."

By war's end ultrapatriotic mobs had seized 1,260 dissenters, driving over 1,100 from their homes. They had tarred and feathered 64, kidnapped and whipped 55, forced 23 to kiss the flag in public, and lynched 4—while authorities looked the other way.

Sanity did not return with the end of the war. The Russian Revolution of 1917 had alarmed Attorney General A. Mitchell Palmer. He viewed all American radicals, especially those originally from Europe, as dangerous revolutionaries. Whipping up anti-alien hysteria in the press, he encouraged veterans to break up May Day workers' parades.

When the IWW opened a union branch in Centralia, Washington, a mob of veterans attacked its hall. They smashed windows and broke down the door; running riot through the building, they destroyed everything. Besieged workers opened fire on the mob, killing four rioters.

The legionnaires seized local IWW leader Wesley Everest. They beat and kicked him, smashing his face with rifle butts. Police arrested and jailed him for the shootings. A hostile mob broke into the Centralia jail and dragged him out. They drove him to a bridge and hanged him from a girder. Then they riddled his body with bullets and threw his corpse into the river.

THE PALMER RAID RIOTS

Attorney General Palmer decided to make a mass roundup of known and suspected radicals, especially the foreign born. He appointed his young protégé J. Edgar Hoover to organize a new unit that eventually became the Federal Bureau of Investigation (FBI). On New Year's Day, 1920, federal agents, soon called G-men (for Government men), made simultaneous raids on workers' homes and offices in thirty-three cities all over the United States. They arrested over ten thousand workers.

The next day Palmer had to release sixty-five hundred for lack of evidence. All but a few of the rest were freed shortly after.

In Boston a mob of five hundred of Palmer's deputized super-patriots burst into union halls. They lined everyone up to be searched, then illegally dragged six hundred workers off to jail for interrogation. In Lynn, Massachusetts, they handcuffed, chained, and hauled off to jail thirty-nine people who had met to organize a co-op. Their objective was as much anti-union as allegedly antisubversive.

In Detroit police held eight hundred workers for one week in a filthy, windowless jail corridor with one toilet and no sinks, without pressing any charges against them.

The *New Republic* charged that Palmer's raiders were "a governmental mob" engaged in a "colossal conspiracy against constitutional rights." Many workers caught up in the Palmer raids were non-Marxist immigrants with no knowledge of their civil rights under the Constitution.

A committee of distinguished lawyers headed by Professor Felix Frankfurter, later a Supreme Court justice, branded Palmer's use of deputized mobs for his raids illegal. Federal Judge George W. Anderson agreed, and he stopped all government deportation of "undesirables." By that time, however, the mobs had put 240 alien radicals on board ships bound for Russia.

Nearly every ethnic, religious, or racial minority that has stepped off a boat or plane onto our shores has come under mob attack at one time or another. They include Catholics, Jews, Africans, Asians, Irish, Italians, Mexicans, Central Americans, and others. Perceived as "different," they have been resented and often hated, especially as they competed for jobs, housing, welfare, medical care, and schooling for their children. Those who succeed in America are often envied, stirring the wrath of Americans at the bottom of the economic ladder.

Ironically, when minority groups become strong and united

enough, they may lash back at oppressors with riots of their own. Participation in such mobs is a means of expressing anger, rebelliousness, and desire for revenge. It also establishes pride of identity in race, religion, or cult. Rioting gives traditional underdogs a new, heady sense of power, as they become aware that they can strike fear into the hearts of those who have oppressed them—and thus continue the cycle of violence.

THREE

When Racial Prejudice Creates Violence

A rumor swept Boston that George Thompson, a British abolitionist, would be guest speaker at a Boston Female Anti-Slavery Society meeting in Anti-Slavery Hall. Handbills flooded the city offering one hundred dollars "...raised by a number of patriotic citizens to reward the individual who shall first lay violent hands on Thompson, so that he may be brought to the tar-kettle."

William Lloyd Garrison, editor of the abolitionist paper the *Liberator*, knew that Thompson was out of town. On October 21, 1835, he offered to speak in Thompson's place, despite threats by a mob of Boston truckdrivers to tar and feather, then kill him if he did.

Arriving at Anti-Slavery Hall, he found a mob of about a hundred men milling about the building entrance. Another hundred lined two flights of stairs up to the third-floor hall.

He pushed his way through the crowded stairs without being recognized. Entering the hall, he took a seat beside another abolitionist guest speaker, C. C. Burleigh. They were the only men among twenty-five women.

A cry went up the staircase: "That was Garrison!"

The mob grew increasingly surly. Some men pushed their way

into the hall. Behind them the surging crowd rapidly grew to several thousand. They ripped the downstairs door off its hinges and thrust more rioters into the hall.

A roar went up for Garrison to be turned over to the mob.

Mary Parker, president of the society, grew frightened for his safety. At her pleading, Garrison and Burleigh retreated into an adjacent office and locked the door.

The women opened the meeting with a prayer, asking God to forgive the rioters besieging them. Mayor Theodore Lyman arrived, escorted by a few policemen. He tried to quell the uproar and disperse the mob, but the rioters paid no attention to him or the police. They ripped down and smashed the society's sign, roaring, "We must have Garrison! Out with him! Lynch him!"

Some of the mob, searching the hall for him, began kicking in the lower panel of the locked office door. They spotted Garrison sitting at a desk, calmly writing a news story about the riot for his antislavery paper.

"There's Garrison! Out with the scoundrel!"

He escaped out a back window by dropping onto a roof shed. But the mob below spotted him. Rioters climbed out after him, pursuing him into an upper story of a carpenter's shop. When they seized him, the roaring crowd in the street yelled, "Throw him out the window!"

One rioter inside put a rope around Garrison's neck. Two others prepared to hang him from the windowsill.

"No, wait a minute," a fourth urged. "Don't let us kill him outright. Let's give him a coat of tar and feathers first, and put a black dye on his face and hands. Then we'll have him in his true colors!"

Roaring with laughter, the men slipped the noose from Garrison's neck to down around his waist. They forced him to climb down a ladder that the mob had brought up. Rioters ripped off his trousers, tore his coat to shreds, and stripped the shirt from his body. The hooting mob put the rope around his neck and dragged him through the streets.

Garrison stumbled along in the center of the human storm. Men ran alongside, taunting him and spitting in his face.

He kept his head up, refusing to show fear.

"THEY'RE GOING TO HANG HIM!"

They're going to hang him!" a spectator cried out to Mayor Lyman. "For God's sake, save him!"

The mayor managed to relay orders to two burly truck-business owners. They smashed their way to Garrison's side. Seizing him roughly, they cast aside the rope. Then they rushed him to the mayor's office. The mob howled in dismay. In City Hall the half-naked abolitionist leader was given a coat, a hat, and a pair of pants. The mob uproar outside continued.

Lyman proposed taking Garrison to jail, a mile away. It was the only place in Boston he would be safe from the mob. Garrison agreed to be arrested on a technical charge of "disturbing the peace." To avoid the rioters outside still howling for his blood, the mayor whisked him away through a back entrance into a carriage.

The mob spotted the escape. Hanging on to the carriage wheels, rioters forced open the doors, grabbed the horses, and tried to overturn the vehicle. Police rushed to tear them off. The horses flew at full gallop until they reached the safety of the jail.

Despite the threats against his life, the courageous Garrison stood firmly by his convictions. In the morning he commemorated the occasion with an inscription on the jail wall:

WM. LLOYD GARRISON WAS PUT INTO THIS CELL WEDNESDAY AFTERNOON, OCTOBER 21, 1835, TO SAVE HIM FROM THE VIOLENCE OF A "RESPECTABLE AND INFLUENTIAL" MOB, WHO SOUGHT TO DESTROY HIM FOR PREACHING THE ABOMINABLE AND DANGEROUS DOCTRINE THAT "ALL MEN ARE CREATED EQUAL," AND THAT ALL OPPRESSION IS ODIOUS IN

THE SIGHT OF GOD. . . . READER, LET THIS INSCRIPTION REMAIN TILL THE LAST SLAVE IN THIS DESPOTIC LAND BE LOOSED FROM HIS FETTERS.

Garrison's words were still there when the jail was torn down seventeen years later. But the slave system had still to be toppled.

The anti-Garrison riot was significant in that it took place *in the North*. Millions of northerners, as well as southerners, opposed abolition. New England shipowners benefited from transporting enslaved Africans to the South. And during this time three New England states introduced bills to ban antislavery publications. Many northerners worried about offending "our southern friends" by tolerating the activities of "dangerous radicals" like the abolitionists. Besides, most northerners of that day were prejudiced against blacks. They felt so strongly about the issue that they rioted against abolitionists constantly.

Mobs opposing abolition were able to delay emancipation for many years. But eventually the justice of freedom for enslaved Africans prevailed, even though it took a civil war to achieve it.

WHEN ENSLAVED BLACKS RIOTED

Long before white mobs were rioting against abolitionists to keep blacks in slavery, black mobs rioted against white slaveowners. The slave trade had brought black Africans to the United States's North and South until 1808, when slave importations were forbidden. But nothing was done to free the enslaved people who were already here, except when individual slaveowners decided to emancipate their own slaves.

In 1712 a mob of enslaved Africans in New York City armed themselves with guns, pistols, swords, daggers, knives, and hatchets. Setting fire to several buildings, they murdered or wounded sixteen whites who sought to put out the blazes.

The Africans fled before a militia that pursued them. Six committed suicide rather than surrender. Twenty-seven others were captured, and twenty-one of the captives were either burned alive, hanged, or tortured to death.

A mob of captive Africans in South Carolina attacked and burned an armory at Stono in 1739. Then they marched south toward Florida, attacking plantations along the way. They killed thirty whites before a militia company killed or captured most of them.

Two years later another New York City mob of enslaved Africans revolted and set fires that almost burned down the city. They chanted a song: "Usurp the white masters and the city will be ours / Fire! Fire! Torch! Torch! / From all their sins the masters will scorch!" A dozen people were caught and burned alive at the stake.

In 1811 five hundred enslaved blacks at a plantation north of Louisiana revolted and killed two whites, seized arms, and burned several plantations. Hundreds more joined the mob as they began marching to New Orleans. White residents fled before them. U.S. troops who were rushed to subdue the uprising killed eighty-three of the rebels.

Later sixteen were executed in New Orleans. Police mounted their heads on poles along the Mississippi River as a grim warning to all the others.

These uprisings gave the lie to the insistence of slave owners that the enslaved Africans were happy and content.

Whites also rioted against blacks. In 1829 free blacks were flocking to the booming city of Cincinnati. Some northern whites grew incensed at sympathizers for harboring those who had escaped slavery. A white mob raided the black district, burned homes, and killed residents indiscriminately. Half the city's black population—over a thousand men, women, and children—was forced across the border into Canada.

THE KU KLUX KLAN

The South's loss of the Civil War and the emancipation of enslaved blacks infuriated many white southerners. The most prejudiced of them, who were usually also the most ignorant and brutal, organized into the Ku Klux Klan. Their hooded mobs sought to terrorize southern blacks and whites who had come south to help the African-Americans. Klansmen hated blacks and bitterly resented their freedom and rise to positions of equality and power, especially because most Klansmen held jobs low on the professional scale.

Klan mobs threatened, flogged, and tortured blacks into staying away from the polls and giving up their political organizations. They often murdered those who resisted.

Klan mobs also beat, assassinated, or drove out of the state northern whites who risked excursions into the countryside, away from the protection of the federal troops occupying the South. The Klan hounded "unpatriotic scalawags"—southerners who dared oppose the Klan—out of the South by ostracism, arson, and physical attacks.

The Klan grew in numbers until the height of its power in the 1920s and included many prominent politicians as members, as its message of hatred of blacks, as well as of Jews and Catholics, won over millions of prejudiced Americans.

RACE RIOTS IN THE NORTH

In 1917, during and after World War I, race riots broke out in the North when large numbers of southern black field hands migrated to northern cities to escape miserable lives as sharecroppers. Many were hired as strikebreakers. Most did not understand labor issues, but even those who did understand took the jobs—just as Chinese strikebreakers had done earlier—out of economic necessity.

In East St. Louis, unionized white workers went out on strike against an aluminum plant in the summer of 1917. White strikers were already upset by the influx of southern blacks into their city. The union lost the strike, precipitating one of the bloodiest race riots in American history.

White mobs raided the city's ghetto. They drove through at top speed, shooting into African-American homes. An armed mob of blacks sought to keep out all whites attempting to enter their district. Opening fire on two white policemen in a squad car, they killed them both.

Police went berserk. They rioted and attacked every African-American in sight. A white mob of three thousand joined them, crying out for vengeance. Rioters pulled blacks from streetcars, clubbing, kicking, and shooting them. They set homes ablaze and fired at men, women, and children as they ran out. The governor rushed National Guard troops to restore order.

"I saw the mob robbing the homes of Negroes and then set fire to them," testified one black victim, 26-year-old Beatrice Deshong. "The soldiers stood with folded arms and looked on as the houses burned. . . . The police and the soldiers were assisting the mob to kill Negroes and to destroy their homes. I saw the mob hang a colored man to a telegraph pole and riddle him with bullets. . . . They were as vile as they could be."

The death toll rose to forty-eight known dead, with hundreds injured. Many stunned blacks fled to the farms and small towns they had come from. Others moved across the river to St. Louis.

A congressional investigation held the commander of the troops responsible for the riot. It noted that the troops had "fraternized with the mob, joked with them, and made no serious effort to restrain them." The police were also blamed because "they shared the lust of the mob for Negro blood. . . . Instead of being guardians of the peace they became part of the mob . . . adding to the terrifying scenes of rapine and slaughter."

But prosecutors dropped all charges against the police in a deal whereby three officers agreed to plead guilty of rioting. They were fined a token fifty dollars each, paid for by the police force. Only four white rioters were indicted for the murder of forty-eight blacks. But eleven African-Americans were charged with homicide in the deaths of nine whites.

After World War I ended, over twenty-six serious race riots broke out in different parts of the country. Returning white veterans in the North were angered by the shortage of available jobs and homes. They blamed a large wartime migration of southern blacks into their cities and towns.

CHICAGO BEACHES—BLACKS KEEP OUT!

Racial tension grew so intense that white mobs bombed fifty-eight black homes in Chicago during and just after the war. In July 1919 a major riot developed when a black bather at the lakefront swam into water "reserved" for whites and drowned. Blacks charged he had been stoned by a white man and demanded the suspect's arrest. Instead, police arrested a black—and were attacked by blacks, touching off a week of citywide rioting. Mobs of tough young whites from politically sponsored athletic clubs attacked blacks on the streets with guns and knives. Armed African-American mobs counterattacked. White adults in cars sped through black districts, firing wildly. Black snipers fired back at them from concealed locations.

On the third day of the riots, white servicemen joined a civilian mob in driving blacks from their homes, which they then looted, wrecked, and burned. Seizing some blacks, they beat them unconscious and threw them into the flames. In reprisal a black mob burned forty-nine houses in the white immigrant neighborhood west of the stockyards.

The senseless riots claimed 38 lives—23 black, 15 white—and injured over 537 people. Order was finally restored by three regiments of state militia.

Illinois State Attorney Maclay Hoyne accused the Chicago police of flagrant racial prejudice. They had jailed mostly blacks, while promptly releasing the few whites apprehended. The governor appointed a commission to investigate all causes contributing to the race riots.

The commission criticized the city for its segregated housing, which kept blacks and whites from getting to know each other as individuals. It found that police and courts dispensed unequal justice to blacks and whites. In these respects the commission's findings were similar to a report by the Kerner Commission almost half a century later.

White athletic clubs, the commission charged, were breeding grounds for white hoodlum mobs. It blamed unions for barring blacks and employers for hiring blacks as strikebreakers or as cheap non-union labor.

The commission also blamed blacks for accepting such jobs, without acknowledging that few alternatives were available to them.

RACIAL HATRED AND LYNCHINGS

A 1933 study of southern lynchings found that at least a third of the African-American victims lynched by mobs had been falsely accused of crimes. Over half the incidents had been carried out with local police officers participating.

The end of World War I saw the rise of new lynchings against blacks.

The African-American veterans returning from overseas demanded an end to racial prejudice. Having fought for their country and having been dealt with as equals by the British and French, they expected racial equality at home. Many returning to the South refused to conform to the old Jim Crow rules expected of them.

In the first year after the war, southern white mobs lynched seventy "uppity blacks who forgot their place," as racists liked to explain when justifying their atrocities.

THE ZOOT-SUIT RIOTS

A race riot of a different sort occurred in Los Angeles during World War II. Many Mexican-Americans had found jobs there in the booming defense industry. Latino youths in the *barrios* (Mexican-American neighborhoods) exhibited their new prosperity by wearing an exaggerated style of clothing known as a "zoot suit."

In June 1943 rumors spread through Los Angeles that "zoot-suiters" were assaulting female relatives of servicemen. At the same time rumors circulated in the *barrios* that sailors were molesting and insulting Latina girls. Street brawls broke out between mobs of servicemen and Chicanos. The *Los Angeles Daily News* ran a blatantly inflammatory headline: "Zooters Planning to Attack More Servicemen."

A mob of several thousand soldiers, sailors, and civilians raged through the streets of downtown Los Angeles, beating up every Latino they could find. Breaking into theaters, they ordered the house lights up. Then they dragged Latinos out of their seats into the street, beating them savagely. Anyone wearing a zoot suit was pulled off a streetcar and assaulted; police either stood by or arrested the victims.

The zoot-suit riots ended only when the military declared downtown Los Angeles out of bounds for servicemen.

DETROIT'S "BLOODY WEEK"

Another serious race riot occurred in Detroit two weeks later—on June 20—this time between whites and blacks. Detroit was filled with southerners of both races who had migrated north for defense jobs. Cramped into slums, tents, and trailers, they let their tempers reach a flash point.

Racist demagogues like Father Charles Coughlin and white supremacist Reverend Gerald L. K. Smith inflamed racial friction in the war plants. Coughlin was a Detroit priest who spoke on national radio and spread Hitler's racist ideas. Smith edited magazines called *The American Vindicator* and *The Cross and the Flag*, which promoted worker hatred of blacks and Jews.

In June 1943 a spate of rumors followed a brawl between blacks and whites in Detroit's Belle Isle amusement park. Whites heard that rioting blacks had assaulted a white woman. Blacks heard that white sailors had thrown an African-American woman and her baby into the lake, and that police had beaten black witnesses. Neither rumor proved to have the slightest basis in fact.

Nevertheless, shortly after midnight a white mob began attacking blacks as they emerged from all-night movies in downtown Detroit. In reprisal blacks pulled whites off buses driving through the city's ghetto, then beat them up. Police rushed to the ghetto. They used guns and nightsticks against the blacks, who began smashing the store windows of white merchants.

The police cordoned off the black district, patrolling it in squad cars. They jumped out with drawn revolvers and riot guns, shooting at anyone suspected of looting or burning a store. Some police told suspects, "Run and don't look back," then shot them in the back. They also clubbed black onlookers.

Mobs of the whites swept through the streets wielding iron pipes, clubs, rocks, and knives. Police made no attempt to stop their assaults on blacks, even when the violence occurred in front of City Hall.

Federal troops had to be called in to bring Detroit's "Bloody Week" to an end. Dead were twenty-five blacks and nine whites. The riots had injured over seven hundred people and destroyed over two million dollars' worth of property. Police made fifteen hundred arrests.

The *Detroit News* analyzed the riots, observing, "Southern whites have come in vast numbers, bringing with them their Jim Crow notions of the Negro. Southern Negroes have come here to take jobs which give them for the first time in the lives of many of them a decent wage, and a sense of freedom they have never known before. The embers smouldered a long time . . . a slight incident caused them to burst into flame."

Thurgood Marshall, later a Supreme Court Justice, pointed out that Detroit's white police had "enforced the law with an unequal hand. They used 'persuasion' rather than firm action with white rioters, while against Negroes they used the ultimate in force: nightsticks, revolvers, riot guns, submachine guns, and deer guns." He conceded that many blacks had been looting stores but noted that whites had been burning cars and stabbing and beating blacks. Yet the police had killed seventeen blacks and no whites. "The entire record," Marshall accused, ". . . reads like the story of the Nazi Gestapo."

Mobs often riot when rumors circulate about misdeeds of another racial or ethnic group. Often these rumors are highly exaggerated, or totally unfounded, as they are bound to be when passed from mouth to mouth. This makes no difference to an angry mob whose blood lust is aroused. True or not, the rumors supply rioters with the excuse they need to vent their hostility on a hated, resented, or despised group. The real cause of these riots is racial or ethnic prejudice.

This was readily apparent in the rise of mob violence against African-Americans at the end of World War II.

LYNCHING AFRICAN-AMERICAN VETERANS

Almost every victim of lynching since the war has been a veteran," observed John Gunther in *Inside U.S.A.* "The Negro community is . . . more aggressive in its demand for full citizenship—even in the South—than at any other time in history. Roughly one million Negroes entered the armed services. They . . . learned what their rights were; overseas many were treated decently and democratically by whites for the first time in their lives; the consequent fermentations have been explosive."

In July 1946 a mob of thirty Georgians stopped a car containing two black couples and murdered them. In August a Louisiana mob kidnapped two young blacks and dragged them to the woods. After beating them mercilessly, the rioters killed one by burning him alive with a blowtorch. Local authorities made no arrests, finding "no clues in connection with the reputed mob action."

Such mob violence was not unusual.

That year news reports made President Harry S Truman aware of mob assaults on black World War II veterans in the South. "My God!" he exclaimed. "I had no idea it was as terrible as that. We've got to do something! Whatever my inclinations as a native of Missouri might have been, as president I know this is bad. I shall fight to end evils like this." President Truman's reference to his Missouri "inclinations" was an admission of personal racial prejudice, though as president he realized that racial violence could not be tolerated.

He appointed a committee to study civil rights abuses in the South. But southern congressmen defeated the committee's recommendation for civil rights legislation. Exasperated, Truman sought to set an example for the country by integrating all swimming pools in the nation's capital, a small but symbolic gesture challenging segregation in public facilities. A number of cities followed suit.

Mississippi Congressman John B. Williams wrathfully predicted "bloodshed and race riots." Some white mobs fulfilled his prophecy. The worst occurred in St. Louis, where police permitted white youths to drive blacks out of a park's public pool with baseball bats.

Racists spread a false rumor that a black youth had stabbed a white boy to death. That night over five thousand furious whites stormed to the park, beating every black person in sight.

In Chicago working-class whites were infuriated in June 1951 when Harvey Clark, a black war veteran, tried to move his wife and two children into an all-white apartment building in the suburb of Cicero.

The suburb's racist police force tried to prevent the move. A court injunction, however, forced them to stand aside.

The day after the Clarks moved in, a howling white mob attacked the building. The Clarks' flat was looted and their furniture thrown into the street. Rioters set the furniture afire while police watched passively. The Clarks still refused to leave. The mob returned the next day and wrecked the whole building. The Clarks now were forced to leave.

Governor Adlai E. Stevenson ordered in the National Guard. A federal grand jury indicted Cicero's town president, attorney, and police chief on charges of conspiracy and violation of civil rights. Many townspeople expressed indignation that the government and the state were interfering in what they considered a legitimate expression of community sentiment.

"Riots are most likely to occur," noted Algernon D. Black, chairman of the New York Civilian Complaint Board in 1968, "when new groups immigrate and when their effort to enter the housing market, the job market, and the schools becomes a threat to those who feel that the community is theirs."

Racism was the spur to millions of whites who fled the cities to all-white suburbs outside major cities after World War II. Poorer working-class whites who could not afford to join this exodus felt increasingly alienated from the growing black population. Thus the widening divide between the races added to the likelihood of mob rioting.

"A lot of people important for maintaining stability in inner city neighborhoods have left," observed sociologist William Julius Wilson in 1992, twenty-four years later. "This leaves behind what I call the truly disadvantaged population. As the higher income black and white families depart, you have less stability, and in time you have the potential for a violent uprising if you get the right spark. It didn't shock me that Los Angeles blew up."

THE FREEDOM RIDERS RISK THEIR LIVES

Here they come!" screamed a woman in a yellow dress. "Get those niggers and nigger-lovers!"

On May 20, 1961, a mob of thousands in Montgomery, Alabama, were besieging the Greyhound bus terminal. They wielded metal pipes, baseball bats, and other weapons. The mob surged toward an incoming bus carrying twenty-one black and white college students from the North. These were "Freedom Riders," determined to challenge illegal segregation in interstate bus travel down South.

The Freedom Riders had notified local police in advance and requested protection. But when the bus door swung open, not one officer was in view.

NBC-TV and *Life* magazine photographers began recording the arrival at the terminal. Rioters hurled themselves at the cameramen, smashing their equipment on the ground. The mob seized riders, who tried to enter the terminal, then threw them over a rail into a cement parking lot ten feet below the station.

Those Freedom Riders who were able to get up sought to flee the mob's fury. But the rioters pursued, and they clubbed, punched, or threw the students to the ground. John Seigenthaler, an administrative assistant to Attorney General Robert Kennedy, sent along as an observer, was knocked unconscious.

The mob injured most of the Freedom Riders.

Earlier that month, when riders had been attacked in Birmingham, police arrived too late to prevent violence. "They put fifty stitches in my head and face to put me back together again," said Jim Peck, a Freedom Rider. "When Police Chief Connor was asked why there was not a single policeman at the Birmingham Trailways terminal to avert mob violence, he explained that since it was Mother's Day, most of the police were off-duty visiting their mothers."

In Montgomery the police arrived only when the riot had raged for over ten minutes. They made no effort to render first aid to the injured, but they "called" for an ambulance, which failed to show up. Asked why the ambulance did not appear, Montgomery Public Safety Commissioner L. B. Sullivan shrugged. "It was broken down and could not come," he replied.

Freedom Rider Jim Zwerg, who had been knocked unconscious, declared from his hospital bed, ". . . segregation must be stopped. It must be broken down. Those of us who are in the Freedom Rides will continue. I'm not sure if I'll be able to, but we are going on to New Orleans no matter what happens. We are dedicated to this. We will take hitting. We'll take beatings. We're willing to accept death. But we are going to keep coming until we can ride [from] anywhere in the South to anyplace else in the South, as Americans, without anyone making any comment."

Alabama Governor John Patterson blamed the riot at the bus terminal on the Freedom Riders. "I have no use," he snapped, "for these agitators or their kind!"

The Freedom Riders of the North who volunteered to come south to try to end racial discrimination had known that they would face injury, even death, at the hands of racist white mobs. Many endured the violence out of a conscience that told them black and white Americans should be treated equally under the law.

The struggle took a long time. Eventually, however, their bravery, along with courageous protests by other blacks and whites, helped bring about the civil rights laws that changed the country.

"RACISM IN THE FIRST DEGREE"

On August 23, 1989, an African-American youth, Yusuf Hawkins, 16, visited Bensonhurst, the mostly Italian-American section of Brooklyn, New York, with three friends at 9:30 P.M. They had come to inspect a used car advertised in a local paper.

A mob of local white youths, most of them jobless school dropouts with drug-abuse records, confronted them with baseball bats and a gun. Inflamed by a rumor that a neighborhood Italian-American girl was dating a black man, the white mob attacked the four black youths.

"Club the niggers!" one white teenager shouted.

The African-American teenagers tried to escape but were chased by the mob. Rioter Joseph Fama cornered Yusuf Hawkins with an upraised gun.

"The hell with beating them up!" he cried. He fired four shots. Two hit Hawkins in the chest.

At this the mob scattered. Hawkins lay dying while a local white woman held his hand.

"He was scared," she said later. "He was just a kid."

Three years earlier another white racist mob had similarly attacked and chased three black men who had appeared in the mostly white Howard Beach section of Queens. One of the men, Michael Griffith, fled from the mob in panic onto a busy highway and was killed by a passing car.

The murder of Hawkins in Bensonhurst stunned a city beset by rising racial tensions. According to New York City police, crimes caused by racial prejudice had jumped from 286 in 1985 to over 400 by 1987. A black leader, Reverend Al Sharpton, now led protest marches through Bensonhurst. Taunting white mobs greeted the demonstrators with raised fists.

Inflammatory press coverage added to the racial tension. Apprehension gripped the city when two of the white Bensonhurst attackers went on trial for the murder of Hawkins. Sharpton suggested that if the jury brought in "not guilty" verdicts, that would be "telling us to burn the town down!"

Joseph Fama was tried first and convicted. Next day 19-year-old Keith Mondello, who had confessed to having been a ringleader of the mob attack, went on trial. A jury found him guilty of some lesser charges but not guilty of murder.

The Hawkins family, seated in court, shrieked in dismay. Pointing at the jurors, they shouted, "He *did* it! He *did* it!" Furious black onlookers yelled at Mondello, "You'll get yours! We'll do it ourselves!"

New York Mayor David Dinkins said angrily that Yusuf Hawkins had been killed by "racism in the first degree!"

As night fell, angry mobs of blacks milled around Brooklyn, disrupting traffic and throwing rocks and bottles. Rioters set fires and ran through the streets of Bedford-Stuyvesant and east New York, knocking over trashcans. They looted a store, then assaulted several whites with bricks and two-by-fours. When TV news vans arrived to cover the riot, the mob injured three of the reporters.

Racial intolerance is a profoundly serious problem when members of different races risk their lives simply by passing through each other's neighborhoods. Some observers believe that with more integrated neighborhoods, blacks and whites will become more accepting of each other's presence. But that solution to the problem is still a long way from being realized in this, the last decade of the twentieth century.

On the other hand, progress in race relations *is* being made in the workplace. By 1989 white employees and 799,000 black managers and executives were working side by side, learning to see each other as people, not racial stereotypes.

"My generation," said Ted Childs, a black personnel manager at IBM, "is the first generation to have gone to the ballfield and the classroom together. Our role in life is to get white folks comfortable with black people." When that goal is mutually realized, animosity between the races is likely to diminish.

When Americans Fear Losing Their Jobs

A crowd of up to five thousand poorly clad New Yorkers braved the February cold to attend a protest meeting in front of City Hall.

"Fellow workers," a speaker cried, "we're in a crisis! Two hundred thousand of us in the city are without jobs. Our families are starving! How can we even afford bread when the price of flour has doubled to twelve dollars a barrel? I'm talking about greedy wholesalers like Hart and Company!"

"Right!" shouted another worker. "Those swindlers are hoarding miles of flour and wheat in their warehouse. They're making big profits out of the suffering of the poor!" By limiting the availability of flour—the daily bread of the poor—companies were able to keep the price high.

"Raid their warehouse!" yelled another. "Show them the workers of New York won't stand for having the bread stolen out of the mouths of our families!"

With an angry roar, a mob of thousands charged down Broadway toward the Hart & Company warehouse. Police watching the rally whistled for reinforcements, then raced after the mob.

The year was 1837. Sweeping unemployment had followed in the wake of a financial panic. Inflation had sent rents soaring, along with the prices of food and fuel. Jobless workers demonstrated to demand price controls and the restoration of two hundred thousand New Yorkers to jobs. They had been nonviolent until the day of this protest meeting in front of City Hall.

Now their patience was exhausted.

The mob reached the Hart warehouse and charged inside. Both men and women rioters seized hundreds of barrels of flour and rolled them out into the street. Flour spilled from the smashed barrels, turning rioters' clothes and faces a ghostly white. The mob also pitched thousands of bushels of wheat to the pavement.

Police charged through the ankle-deep flour. But the vandals overwhelmed them and ripped away their nightsticks. New York's mayor arrived simultaneously with the rest of the mob from the park. He begged the rioters to go home.

"What homes?" yelled a worker. "The landlords have been kicking us out because we can't pay the rent!"

The rioters drove the mayor off with a hail of bricks and chunks of ice. Flour was now everywhere. Women scooped it up into boxes, baskets, and aprons, then hurried home with the white treasure to their families.

As night fell, fresh detachments of police arrived, along with military troops. They arrested several rioters. But the mob pursued and fought the police, freeing the prisoners.

The *New York Commercial Register* grimly reminded its affluent readers that the French Revolution had begun with "mobs clamoring for bread, marching in procession, and committing outrages against the bakers."

The Flour Riot frightened wealthy Americans. They saw it as the possible forerunner of a new revolution that would pit the poor masses against the prosperous few. Worried socialites began organizing concerts and balls to raise funds from the wealthy for relief of the poor.

"FIGHT VIOLENCE WITH VIOLENCE!"

Chicago railroad workers of the Pullman Company, which made sleeping cars, were shocked and enraged when company president George Pullman slashed their already low wages by as much as 40 percent. He did so even as his company reported large profits. Pullman awarded company stockholders an 8 percent dividend. Millionaires Cornelius Vanderbilt and Marshall Field were among those who collected.

Pullman workers were already embittered by being compelled to live in the company's "model village," a company town in Pullman, Illinois (later part of Chicago). Workers had to buy everything they needed from the company stores, where goods were overpriced. Over forty-five hundred workers earned an average of $613 a year each, but they were overcharged for rent, gas, and water. Prices charged to them stayed up while the wages paid to them went down.

Workers were in debt to the company for a total of over $70,000—a lot of money in those days. Pullman kept them in debt to tie them to their jobs. If workers couldn't afford to pay cash for goods at the company store, or the cost of rent and utilities, the amounts would be deducted from their paychecks. After such deductions, many received less than fifty cents a week.

"We were born in a Pullman house," one worker said bitterly, "fed from the Pullman shop, taught in the Pullman school, catechized in the Pullman church, and when we die we shall be buried in the Pullman cemetery and go to the Pullman hell!"

The workers chose a grievance committee to appeal to George Pullman to rescind the wage cuts. He fired everyone on the committee.

In desperation three thousand Pullman employees went out on strike. They appealed to Eugene Debs, head of the new American Railway Union (ARU), to help them. The early union movement had arisen to protest oppressive working conditions, low pay, and lack of job security. Industrialists of that day took advantage of unorganized workers to maximize their profits. Unions opposed employers with the threat of striking if union demands were not met.

Debs asked Pullman for arbitration.

"There is nothing to arbitrate," the magnate snapped.

Debs accused him of counting on "a little starvation" to bring his workers to their knees. He ordered ARU members not to handle any trains carrying Pullman sleeping cars.

The year was 1894. The boycott crippled rail operations in twenty-seven states. It virtually paralyzed lines in the Middle and Far West. Angered tycoons of twenty-four railroad lines organized the General Managers' Association (GMA) to come to the aid of Pullman and smash the strike.

The GMA put pressure on Chicago's mayor, John P. Hopkins. He ordered police to break up workers' demonstrations. The GMA also hired two thousand men and had the U.S. marshal make them deputies. The Chicago chief of police himself called them "thugs, thieves, and ex-convicts." Some joined the strikers as spies and agents provocateurs, urging and provoking violence.

The GMA left no stone unturned to crush the strike. It used police, courts, federal troops, Pinkerton detectives, and the two thousand thugs, and they influenced the press.

Newspapers mobilized public opinion against the strike. "War of the bloodiest kind in Chicago is imminent," said the *Washington Post,* "and before tomorrow goes by the railroad lines and yards may be turned into battlefields strewn with hundreds of dead and wounded." Another paper denounced Debs for leading "a war against the government and against society."

Pullman hired strikebreakers and ordered them to provoke fights with striking union members. Company saboteurs pretending to be strikers set fire to obsolete freight cars in the Chicago yards. The press obligingly reported that "insurrection and mob rule by strikers" had created a reign of terror in the city. Papers called for armed troops to shoot down "the lawless mob terrorizing Chicago."

These tactics infuriated the Pullman workers. The once disciplined strikers became what the press had represented them to be—a lawless mob. To stop trains from running, they derailed freight cars, obstructed tracks, threw switches, and pulled strikebreaking engineers off trains.

"Fight violence with violence!" one worker urged. "They don't understand any other language!"

The strikers sidetracked freight trains hauling perishable fruit and other cargoes. They raided the carloads of rotting food, as well as the coal cars, to provision their families. Enraged railroad officials demanded that the militia protect the cargoes with loaded guns.

U.S. Attorney General Richard Olney, an ex-railroad lawyer and railroad director, obtained an unprecedented federal court injunction against the blocking of trains. He pointed out that the mails were being held up. Olney talked President Grover Cleveland into sending federal troops into Chicago to "restore order." The president did so over the protest of Illinois Governor John B. Altgeld, who was disgusted with the brutal tactics of Pullman and the GMA.

Debs refused to call off the strike, despite the injunction. Cavalrymen swinging sabers and infantrymen with fixed bayonets charged a mob of strikers and killed twenty.

Police arrested Debs and other union leaders. They were indicted for "conspiracy to obstruct the mails" and refusing to obey the court injunction. A judge sent Debs to jail for six months, despite Governor Altgeld's appalled protest.

The strike collapsed.

Theodore Roosevelt, then a U.S. Civil Service commissioner, praised President Cleveland's suppression of the strike. The way to handle union radicals, Roosevelt declared, was to take "ten or a dozen leaders out, standing . . . them up against a wall and shooting them dead."

The federal troop riot against the strikers that broke the strike turned Eugene Debs from a labor leader into a Socialist. "The issue is Socialism versus Capitalism," he declared. "I am for Socialism because I am for humanity!" Millions of embittered workers followed him into the new Socialist party and sought to elect Debs president.

His Socialist vote increased in subsequent elections. In his 1918 campaign, Debs denounced America's entry into World War I after President Woodrow Wilson had declared war. He was arrested and sentenced to ten years in jail, from which he continued to run for president. Debs received almost a million votes but was kept in prison until pardoned by President Warren Harding in 1921. He continued to lead the Socialist party until his death five years later.

RIOTS OF THE GREAT DEPRESSION

A mob of five hundred jobless, hungry men and women gathered at City Hall to listen to Floyd Phillips of the Oklahoma City Unemployed Council. He denounced the economic system that denied them work and refused them emergency relief.

Passions aroused, the mob rushed into a nearby grocery store to seize food for themselves and their families. Store manager H. A. Shaw tried to reason with them.

"It's too late to bargain with us!" Phillips shouted.

A police emergency squad rushed to the scene and lobbed tear-gas shells into the mob. Gasping and weeping, rioters who were crushed against each other smashed store windows to escape. Police arrested five women and twenty-six men for rioting.

Mobs of the unemployed were making similar raids on food stores across the country. In Chicago over 40 percent of workers were jobless. A third of the city's million people were in desperate circumstances. Over two hundred poor families a week were being evicted by court orders for being unable to pay their rent.

Mobs of angry sympathizers gathered threateningly when families were dumped out of their homes with no place to go. When the furniture of Mrs. Diana Gross, a 72-year-old Chicago black woman, was put out on the street, an outraged mob of five thousand people, black and white, defied police and bailiffs by carrying the furniture back inside her flat. Three of the mob were arrested. One police officer fired a warning shot.

At that the infuriated mob fell upon the police and beat them mercilessly. Some police fired at rioters, killing three and wounding several others.

Some twenty thousand whites and forty thousand blacks marched grimly in a funeral procession for the dead men. This rare unity of blacks and whites may have occurred because whites as well as blacks suffered evictions during these hard times. During the procession, police heard angry calls for an uprising against the city. Nervous Chicago authorities quickly announced a temporary suspension of all evictions.

The year was 1931. The Great Depression had begun to engulf the whole country. Between 1930 and 1932 over fifteen million Americans lost their jobs. Millions more suffered severe pay cuts. Most states had no unemployment-compensation or public-assistance programs. And there was no Social Security system to benefit people when they retired, providing monthly government payments based on their lifetime payments into the system.

In Chicago a mob of men fought over a restaurant's back door garbage. In Philadelphia a storekeeper kept one family from starving to death by giving them indefinite credit. "Eleven children in that house," he told a reporter. "They've got no shoes, no pants. In the house, no chairs. My God, you go in there, you cry, that's all."

In March 1932 some five thousand jobless auto workers from Detroit marched to the Ford plant in Dearborn, Michigan, to demonstrate against company layoffs. Dearborn police sought to turn them back from the Ford gates. The angry workers rioted, fighting the police hand to hand. Ford firemen knocked down workers with high-speed water hoses. The police hurled tear gas, then opened fire with a machine gun. Four workers were killed and a dozen more badly wounded.

Over thirty-nine thousand sullen workers attended the funeral ceremony for the victims of the Dearborn massacre. The *Detroit Times* declared, "The killing of innocent workmen . . . is a blow directed at the very heart of American institutions."

In February 1933 desperate mobs verged on insurrection. A Seattle mob of thousands seized the county building to demand jobs and welfare payments. In the Blue Ridge Mountains hungry rioters smashed store windows and seized food.

In April 1934 a Minneapolis mob of six thousand fired stones, bottles, and lumps of coal through the windows of City Hall. They demanded government-created jobs and higher welfare payments. The next month the city's teamsters went on strike for union recognition. Business leaders fought them with a deputized "citizens' army." A subsequent clash with twenty thousand teamsters left two men killed on either side and sixty-seven truck drivers wounded. The violence ended only when the teamsters won union recognition.

Violent strikes were waged by streetcar workers in Milwaukee and by cab drivers in Philadelphia and New York. When striking auto-parts workers in Toledo clashed with police, an excited correspondent of the London *Daily Herald* cabled London: "Toledo is in the grip of civil war!"

THE STRUGGLE TO ORGANIZE UNIONS

In city after city, workers rioted in their fight for union recognition. Jobs during the Great Depression were scarce. Because labor was plentiful, employers were able to compel employees to work long hours at low pay. Workers could be fired arbitrarily. Only a union could put pressure on employers to be fair, under threat of a strike.

But employers did not hesitate to use ever greater violence to crush workers' strikes.

Socialist leader Norman Thomas organized ten thousand black and white sharecroppers into the Southern Tenant Farmers Union (STFU). Landlords, planters, and absentee corporations hired armed mobs to attack them, and police deputized these thugs.

The thugs broke up sharecroppers' meetings and jailed STFU members on trumped-up charges. They evicted others from land holdings. Local officials denied the sharecroppers relief payments. The deputized mob riddled their homes with machine-gun fire and burned their churches. "Riding bosses" hunted down STFU organizers. Union members were flogged and murdered.

Forty states issued injunctions against organizing unions, striking, and picketing. Union men who fought back against company-organized mobs were often jailed for "assault with intent to murder." California sheriffs and deputies, in the pay of big landowners, rioted against union attempts to organize thousands of exploited fruit workers.

The New Deal administration of President Franklin D. Roosevelt sought to respond to the turbulence of the depression with acts of social justice. "Change is the order of the day," he promised. His New Deal program introduced the Social Security Act of 1935, providing jobless workers with unemployment insurance and allowing joint contributions from workers and employers to provide old-age benefits. The national government made grants to the states for aid to needy dependent children, crippled children, pregnant women, the aged, and the blind.

Roosevelt declared: "A government that could not care for its old and sick, that could not provide work for the strong, that fed its young into the hopper of industry, and that let the black shadow of insecurity rest on every home, was not a government that could endure or should endure." He called his Social Security program "security from the cradle to the grave."

"Socialism!" screamed critics, largely Republicans, who dreaded government spending for social programs. But they could not dismantle the Social Security program, nor did they dare try. It became a floor of support for the average American family.

And in 1935 the New Deal established a new climate of recognition for labor's rights. The Wagner Labor Relations Act created the National Labor Relations Board (NLRB), giving it the power to compel employers to bargain with unions elected by their employees. The Wagner Act gave tremendous impetus to rapid unionization of the biggest industries in the country.

THE COMPANY GUARDS RIOT
AT REPUBLIC STEEL

The big corporations, however, tried to stonewall efforts to unionize. General Motors workers, tired of company stalling, occupied GM plants in Flint, Michigan, with a sit-down strike that lasted forty-four days. They finally compelled General Motors to sign a labor contract with the United Automobile Workers Union, Congress of Industrial Organizations (CIO).

Other sit-down strikes involving half a million workers won recognition from the rubber, textile, oil-refining, and shipbuilding industries. These victories also led the big steel companies to yield to unionization.

But the "Little Steel" companies, led by Tom Girdler, the tough president of Republic Steel, were another story. They fought their millworkers' struggle for union recognition with espionage, strikebreaking, blacklists, and private armies of thugs wearing company badges.

Republic Steel ignored the Wagner Act, as well as a law prohibiting the importation of strikebreakers across state lines. The company kept its South Chicago plant open with strikebreakers who slept inside the plant, protected by armed guards. Police were paid secretly by

Republic Steel to harass union picket lines. Chicago Mayor Edward Kelly refused to allow more than sixteen picketers at each gate.

Some three thousand strikers defied this ban on Memorial Day, 1937. They and their wives set up a mass picket line in front of Republic's gates. They were orderly for the most part, although some strikers threw stones and sticks at cars speeding strikebreakers through the picket lines.

At the end of the day many strikers and their wives began walking toward their parked cars to leave for home. Suddenly armored trucks shot out from the main plant entrance. About three hundred uniformed company guards, heavily armed, leapt out of the trucks in the middle of the street.

They hurled tear gas and fired guns point-blank at the dispersing workers and their families. People scattered in panic, screaming. The guard mob chased them, firing guns and clubbing down men and women in the gutter.

Workers fell, groaning. Guards charged over the dead and wounded to club and shoot down those who fled. The guards continued rioting into a street full of spectators. The hail of gunfire caught a group of children returning from school. From the roof of a Republic Steel building other company guards fired tear-gas bombs, adding to the terror and confusion in the street.

The guards killed ten workers, shooting six in the back. Ninety more workers and spectators were injured.

Mayor Kelly's police chief rushed to the defense of the company. He insisted that it had been necessary to open fire on a "bloodthirsty armed mob led by outside agitators and Communists." Although not a single demonstrator was proved to have a gun, the pro-corporation Chicago press echoed his charges.

Senator Robert La Follette led a Senate investigation of the Memorial Day massacre. "It was almost beyond description, Senator," testified eyewitness Darrell C. Smith. "It was just about the bloodiest scene possible. . . . I saw women struck with those iron bars just as mercilessly as though they were men. I saw a group of schoolchildren across the street running around in a panic, scared, crying at the top of their lungs because they were frightened out of their wits by this tear-gas shooting that was going on all around them. These guards were rushing around the people, and beating the people to the brick pavement, and then beating them after they were down."

The steelworkers learned that Paramount Pictures had made a newsreel of the riot. They demanded that the film be released. Paramount executives refused, claiming it might "incite local riot and perhaps riotous demonstrations." But Senator La Follette subpoenaed the film for his committee.

Committee members were shocked by the scenes of the company guards rioting. "We think it plain that the force employed by the police," the committee reported, "was far in excess of that which the occasion required . . . a deliberate effort to intimidate the strikers." Over half a century later another film of police out of control shocked the nation, in the Rodney King case.

The committee learned that Little Steel—Republic Steel and other small steel companies—had seven thousand guards, patrolmen, deputy sheriffs, national guardsmen, city police, and company police on its payroll for antistrike duty. The company had spent over $4 million to crush the strike, using $141,000 worth of munitions in the process.

The Memorial Day massacre marked the last gasp of diehard industrialists to smash union labor. Soon afterward Little Steel, too, was under union contract.

When Americans fear for their jobs, or are ruthlessly exploited, or lose their jobs, desperation may lead them to riot. Corporations determined to resist union demands and to break strikes violently have sometimes hired mobs to provoke violence.

Labor riots such as these forced shocked Americans to face the injustice suffered by workers. They led eventually to the passage of the Wagner Act, compelling industrialists to bargain with unions. Turmoil in the streets underlined the seriousness of the Depression and hastened the introduction of the New Deal and a new social environment for change.

FIVE

When Police Turn Violent

On a freezing January morning over seven thousand immigrant workers and their families jammed into Tompkins Square Park in New York City. They carried signs reading: WE DEMAND PUBLIC WORKS JOBS. . . . STOP UNFAIR PAY CUTS. . . . STOP EVICTING JOBLESS WORKERS FROM THEIR HOMES. . . . GIVE PUBLIC RELIEF TO THE HUNGRY.

An economic depression had thrown hundreds of thousands of Americans out of work. It had slashed the wages of millions of workers. Socialists, reformers, and union members had formed a workers' Committee of Safety to petition City Hall for public assistance.

New York City officials had refused to meet with the committee, whose members then planned a huge protest march through the city. But the police refused to give them a permit—"to avoid annoyance to the business community and the public."

The angry committee then called the great protest rally in Tompkins Square Park. When thousands of workers and their families filled the park, committee speakers prepared to air labor's grievances and urge a general strike.

Suddenly a detachment of police stormed into the park. Without a word of warning they swept down on the defenseless demonstrators.

The first to fall under their onslaught was a woman carrying a protest banner. The police used their clubs left and right on the heads of all demonstrators within reach. Women and children screamed as they were crushed back upon one another in a wild scramble to escape the nightsticks.

Mounted police galloped into the crowd repeatedly, using their horses as weapons. They rode down men, women, and children indiscriminately. Thousands fled out of the park in panic, pursued by the police into adjacent streets. Horrified spectators watched the orgy of brutality.

"I was caught in the crowd on the street," labor leader Samuel Gompers reported, "and barely saved my head from being cracked by jumping down a cellarway. The attacks of the police kept up all day long—wherever the police saw a group of poorly dressed persons. . . . The next few days disclosed revolting stories of police brutality inflicted on the sick, the lame, the innocent bystander. . . . To this day I cannot think of that wild scene without my blood surging in indignation."

But New York Police Commissioner Abram Duryee was delighted with the rioting of his force. "It was the most glorious sight I ever saw, the way the police broke and drove the crowd," he gloated. "Their order was perfect as they charged with their clubs uplifted."

It was 1874. The press, then controlled by big-business interests, praised the police for their suppression of the "troublemakers" and denounced the unemployed for their "Communistic spirit." One paper insisted that if another protest rally were held, the city should again "club it to death at the hands of the police, or shoot it to death at the hands of the militia."

A year earlier, illicit stock-market manipulation by officials of the administration of President Ulysses S. Grant had brought about a financial panic. A severe business depression had followed. Police beat and arrested those who demonstrated against unemployment and high prices.

Neither the police involved in the Tompkins Square Park riot nor Commissioner Duryee were called to account for their brutal attacks on defenseless workers. Consequently they felt free to invade and break up all private labor meetings.

"The police," noted Samuel Gompers, "frustrated several meetings held to protest brutality, and in defense of the right of free assemblies for a lawful purpose."

Police arrested strikers on picket lines, beat them, and held them without charges. They also looked the other way when hired company thugs attacked strikers. Police riots frightened so many workers away from unions that soon there was only one unionized cigar shop left in New York City.

Police Commissioner Duryee denied trade union leaders' charges that his police were rioting like a mob. He insisted that whatever violence they used was necessary to "suppress Communism."

The police rarely arrested company hirelings who beat, shot, and killed labor organizers, radicals, and strikers. One reason was that most police of that era were intensely antilabor. They reflected the views of department chiefs, judges, and politicians who owed their appointments or election to campaign contributions from the corporations and big businessmen.

"KILL! KILL! KILL!"

Tompkins Square Park became the scene of another police riot more than a hundred years later. By then it had become an encampment for homeless people. On August 7, 1988, a cordon of 450 police in riot gear suddenly swept into the park. Some of the homeless began to chant, "The park belongs to the people!"

Some police responded with a chant of their own—"Kill! Kill! Kill!"—and began driving the homeless out of the park. Some youths tried to resist, wielding sticks and throwing bottles. The police cracked every head they could reach, and they smashed bicycles. Innocent bystanders were bloodied.

Over three dozen people had to be hospitalized. Police arrested nine. Twenty-seven people filed complaints of police brutality.

In both of these cases the police rioted against the poor and dispossessed, seeking to drive them out of Tompkins Square Park. Even if the police were simply following orders to clear the park, they could have done so peacefully. That they acted violently indicated a strong prejudice against the jobless, the homeless, and the poor.

POLICE RIOTS AGAINST COLORADO MINERS

Ten thousand Colorado miners, long oppressed by Blaine and other mine companies, went on strike for union recognition. The companies imported mobs of armed thugs to reinforce the mine field's small private police force. A local sheriff in southern Colorado deputized the thugs, giving them police powers. The companies issued their first order—to evict strikers from company homes in Telluride, Colorado City, and Cripple Creek.

Mobs of police and thug deputies drove workers and their families out of their homes at gunpoint. The evicted strikers moved into tent colonies set up at Ludlow, Colorado, on land rented by their union. The police mobs then raided the tent colonies to drive the workers out of there. Now angry miners defended themselves with guns. Blazing gun battles killed men on both sides.

To drive strikers away from the mine fields, the companies sent police to attack them in an armored train the executives called the Death Special. The miners learned of this plan and ambushed the train before it reached Ludlow. They shot the engineer and forced the train to retreat.

Colorado Governor Elias Ammons called out the National Guard. He assured the strikers that the guardsmen would protect them from company assaults, and they agreed to surrender their guns. No sooner had they done this than the guardsmen were recalled and replaced by the thug deputies, led by an antilabor officer, Lieutenant K. E. Linderfelt.

"By April 20 the Colorado National Guard no longer offered even a pretense of fairness or impartiality," reported George P. West of the U.S. Commission on Industrial Relations, "and its units in the field had degenerated into a force of professional gunmen and adventurers . . . dominated by an officer whose intense hatred for the strikers had been demonstrated."

On April 20, 1914, Linderfelt led his police mob in an unprovoked attack on the Ludlow tent colony with rifles and a machine gun. The mob killed five men and a boy and set the tents afire. Hundreds of miners and their families fled, pursued by flying bullets. The fires burned or suffocated to death two women and eleven children who had huddled fearfully in the tents.

"During the firing of the tents," West noted, "the militiamen became an uncontrolled mob and looted the tents of everything that appealed to their fancy. . . ."

The police mob took three strike leaders prisoner and shot them. The mine fields erupted in a roar of hatred and rebellion against the authority of the state. Union leaders called on all Colorado workers to arm themselves for revenge.

Mobs of furious strikers attacked mine after mine. They drove off or killed the guards and took possession of the mines. They set fire to some buildings and used dynamite to blow up others, leaving them masses of twisted wreckage. Racing from site to site, they blew up mines, smelters, mine officials, mine operators, and strikebreakers alike.

Ten days of fighting saw another fifty-three people killed.

"This rebellion," reported West, "constituted perhaps one of the nearest approaches to civil war and revolution ever known in this country in connection with an industrial conflict."

Appalled, President Woodrow Wilson finally ordered federal

troops to the mine fields to restore order. The troops stopped the violence by mobs of strikers and mobs of company-deputized police.

Wilson appealed to the Colorado mine owners to bring about industrial peace by recognizing the miners' union. Instead the mine owners pressed prosecution of union leaders. One was convicted of murder, but the Colorado Supreme Court overturned the verdict. Neither the mine owners, Lieutenant Linderfelt, nor any of his police mobs were compelled to answer for the crimes of the Ludlow massacre, which took place from 1913 to 1914.

In the long run the riots on the mine fields made inevitable a public demand for industrial peace. But it wasn't until the 1930s that labor achieved the right to bargain on equal terms with management. Then the stormy class struggle subsided, and the threat of revolution disappeared.

"THE WHOLE WORLD IS WATCHING!"

Perhaps the bloodiest police riot in American history occurred in Chicago. The Democratic National Convention had assembled to nominate Hubert Humphrey as its presidential candidate. He had infuriated opponents of the unpopular Vietnam War by supporting it. The antiwar movement prepared huge demonstrations for Chicago's Lincoln Park.

Chicago Mayor Richard Daley was determined to keep antiwar demonstrators from spoiling Humphrey's nomination. He turned the city into an armed camp, ringing the convention hall amphitheater with barbed wire and barricades, like a fortress. Police protected every entrance. They chased away demonstrators who sought to picket the convention.

Daley mobilized Illinois national guardsmen to assist his blue-helmeted police force. President Lyndon B. Johnson also kept army troops and armored personnel carriers standing by.

The *New York Times* noted, "The Convention thus became, before it even convened, the first national political convention in memory to require the protection of troops."

These police and military preparations frightened thousands of anti–Vietnam War protesters into staying away. Nevertheless, over ten thousand determined demonstrators from all walks of life came to Chicago, representing twenty-four different organizations. They included homemakers, clergy, teachers, Quakers, draft resisters, and hippies.

It was August 28, 1968. Dozens of reporters covered the protest activities. Mayor Daley denounced the demonstrators as "hoodlums and Communists." He sought to disperse them by sending his police to attack them when they gathered in Lincoln Park near the convention hall.

Wearing gas masks, police hurled tear-gas canisters into the crowds. Then they raced after the coughing, gagging demonstrators, clubbing them down. The police also beat ministers and onlookers who sought to protect the fallen.

A squad car drove into one group. A few furious demonstrators yelled, "Kill the cops!" The officer at the wheel of the squad car escaped their wrath by charging the car through the crowds, siren whining, blue light flashing.

Two assistant U.S. district attorneys later reported that the police were in a "state of excited anger. . . . They wanted to bust the heads of the demonstrators."

When police beat youths to the ground, they kept clubbing them. The crowds booed. A warning chant arose: "The whole world is watching! The whole world is watching!" TV and news photographers kept filming the rioting police, who turned and attacked them, smashing their cameras.

Police shoved, chased, struck, and teargassed innocent bystanders and onlookers, along with demonstrators. Their violence raged all through the morning hours. When it ended, the police had caused about one hundred casualties among civilians, including seventeen reporters. Fifteen policemen were treated for injuries.

All week long scenes of violence swirled across the nation's TV sets. They showed young and old people alike being attacked, clubbed, and dragged bleeding into police vans.

Thousands of the demonstrators defied these attacks and attempts to drive them out of Chicago. They sat down in the park instead, chanting the anti–Vietnam War slogan, "Hell, no—we won't go!" Police charged wildly among the sitting protesters, clubbing those on the ground and those seeking to flee.

Weeping people hurt in the crush cried for help. Police cracked heads left and right, kicking victims as they crumpled. People who tried to shield fallen friends were also clubbed and kicked. Police arrested demonstrators by dragging them along the ground while hitting them with nightsticks. Youths with long hair were singled out for the severest beatings.

Reporter Nora Sayre declared, "I saw seven policemen beating one girl—long after she had fallen; a row of sitting singers whose heads were cracked open by a charge of running cops. One medic wearing a white coat and Red Cross armband was grabbed and beaten to the ground, his face bloodied."

A well-dressed woman passerby indignantly protested the officers' unnecessary brutality in arresting demonstrators. An officer sprayed Mace in her face and clubbed her to the ground. Then he and two other policemen dragged her by her arms to a paddy wagon and threw her in bodily.

Nearby, police on motorcycles charged directly into a crowd, creating panic as they knocked people down and ran over them. Some victims were the demonstrators' small children.

"A POLICE RIOT"

Inside the convention hall Senator Abraham Ribicoff became aware of what was going on outside. From the rostrum he denounced Mayor Daley for using "Gestapo tactics." Purple with rage, Daley shouted back a profane defiance.

Angry protests by many important Democratic leaders at the convention eventually compelled Daley to withdraw all police from the demonstrators' gatherings. But by the time the "Battle of Chicago" was over, it had caused 700 civilian and 192 police injuries. Over 400 demonstrators had needed first aid for the effects of tear gas and Mace, and over 100 required hospitalization as a result of other injuries.

Police had jailed almost 700 demonstrators. Out of 300 reporters covering the convention and demonstrations, 65 had been either injured or arrested or had had their cameras smashed. The Chicago Newspaper Guild charged that the police had "conspired with each other to wage planned mayhem on men serving as the public's eyes and ears."

Thomas Pew, Jr., editor of the Troy, New York, *Daily News*, declared that only the presence of TV cameras had prevented the police riot from becoming a massacre. "If they did this while the whole world was watching," he asked, "what might they have done if they had been off camera?"

The final verdict on the 1968 Chicago violence was pronounced by President Johnson's own National Commission on the Causes and Prevention of Violence. Its Walker Report summed up its findings by bluntly describing the events in Chicago as a "police riot."

Yet not a single Chicago police officer was indicted for assaulting reporters, innocent bystanders, and demonstrators who were exercising their First Amendment rights.

U.S. Attorney General Ramsey Clark declared, "There was no need for police violence in Chicago. It did not maintain order, enforce law, prevent crimes, or protect lives and property. It did the opposite. . . . Hundreds of thousands of young people . . . have seen a raw demonstration of police capacity for violence, and they will never forget it."

And they didn't. Student alienation from government increased after the deplorable events in Chicago.

The Chicago police apparently believed the long-haired demonstrators were dangerous agitators against whom total force was both necessary and justified. The demand for "law and order" from a public grown weary of the political uproars in the 1960s supported police savagery against "disturbers of the peace."

The violence in Chicago did not have the effect that Mayor Daley intended. (*Newsweek* called the riot "Daley's gift to Richard Nixon.") The riot soured voters on the Democratic party, and they elected Republican Richard Nixon to the White House. Some voters believed Nixon's promise to end the Vietnam War quickly. Others voted for him in a backlash against the upsetting demonstrations.

Opinion polls found that most Americans who had watched the police riots on TV were sickened by them. Ironically, they were angry not at the brutal police but at the TV networks for showing them this violence. And they preferred to blame the youthful demonstrators who had been attacked rather than the police who had rioted against them.

Twenty-two years later the public came around to recognizing that police brutality was a fact of life for many citizens. By the end of 1991 the city of Los Angeles had paid an estimated thirteen million dollars to settle lawsuits filed against its police department for the use of "excessive force."

Black Congressman John Conyers declared in 1992, "There is a culture of violence that has swept the nation's police forces." A majority of Americans now agreed. A *Newsweek* poll in March 1991 revealed that 62 percent of those polled believed that minority groups were suffering at the hands of police.

When Taxes Become Oppressive

There's one of the scoundrels! *Get him!*"

An angry mob of Boston dockworkers and street toughs had gathered in front of the Custom House, where a soldier was pacing while on guard duty. A group of jeering boys began throwing thick icicles at the guard, Private Hugh White. He threatened them with the butt of his rifle. The rioters brandished clubs and rushed to attack him. White aimed his gun at the mob and shouted for the rest of the guard to turn out.

Other soldiers ran out of the barracks. Fixing their bayonets, they prodded the mob back. Captain Thomas Preston, officer of the day, urged the mob to disperse and go home.

Church bells rang out an alarm. Bostonians turned out of their homes and began running toward Custom House Square, swelling the infuriated mob. Captain Preston posted eight of the armed soldiers on King Street in a semicircle around the Custom House.

The rioters taunted them. "Fire!" one man jeered. "Fire! We dare you!"

The soldiers aimed their guns. The mob pressed the bayonets aside, defying the guards. The rioters knocked one soldier to the ground; he regained his feet and fired into the mob. The other soldiers then fired their guns. Up to a dozen shots rang out, killing three rioters and wounding two.

The rioters fled the square in panic. The soldiers hastily retreated to their barracks. Some rioters ran back to carry off the casualties. One of the dead was a black man, Crispus Attucks.

An infuriated mob of five thousand Bostonians bore down on the soldiers' barracks. The leveled guns of a whole regiment forced them to halt. But the sullen mob refused to disperse until Lieutenant Governor Thomas Hutchinson, who had rushed to the scene, addressed them. He promised that those responsible for the shootings would be brought to trial.

The date was March 5, 1770. The soldiers attacked by the Boston rioters were British redcoats, who controlled the city.

Samuel Adams, an unsuccessful lawyer and businessman turned politician, had skillfully fanned colonial outrage against the British. He had organized the Sons of Liberty and agitated several mobs into anti-British actions.

Adams magnified the Custom House riot that had begun as a street brawl into what became known as the Boston Massacre. He kept passions stirred by melodramatic references to Boston dogs "greedily licking human BLOOD in King Street." He succeeded in infuriating all the colonies over this "military outrage against peace-loving citizens."

Adams's agitation forced a trial of Captain Preston and his eight guards before a Boston jury. They were defended by a future American president, Sam Adams's cousin John Adams.

"I saw the people in great commotion," Preston testified at the trial, "and heard them use the most cruel and horrid threats against the troops. . . . They immediately surrounded the sentinel posted, and with clubs and other weapons threatened to execute their vengeance on him."

The jury of colonists exonerated all but two soldiers. Found guilty of manslaughter, these two were punished by being branded on the hand.

Sam Adams arranged to have March 5 declared an annual day of mourning for those killed at the Custom House. He provided tolling church bells, lighted picture displays of "the Horrid Massacre," and rabble-rousing oratory.

He flooded the colonies with engravings by silversmith Paul Revere that showed a grinning British officer waving his sword to signal a point-blank volley of redcoat rifle fire at twenty peaceful, respectable citizens. His booklet *A Short Narrative of the Horrid Massacre in Boston* whipped up a revolutionary fervor with a lurid, highly colored account of the brawl on King Street.

A calmer, if still biased, appraisal of the affair appeared merely as a footnote in a British book published ten years later, *An Impartial History of the War in America*. The affair was described simply as "an alarming riot in Boston between the soldiers and the inhabitants."

SAM ADAMS, MASTER RABBLE-ROUSER

Each year until the Revolutionary War began, Sam Adams held Fifth of March demonstrations to remind colonists of their first "martyrs." He also established "committees of correspondence" in each of the colonies. These relayed all local grievances against the British to each other, intensifying national indignation. Colonial mobs rioted against the British with increasing frequency in the six years before the revolution.

Sam Adams's agitation spurred the colonies to build and train their militia for defense. This militia later became the nucleus of George Washington's revolutionary army.

The spark that had set off the Boston riots was the occupation of the city by British troops. But the real tinder was economic protest against "taxation without representation."

In 1764 the British had passed the Sugar Act, taxing the colonists' imports of molasses, rum, food, and lumber. Then in 1765 they had passed the Stamp Act, to raise money to support royal troops quartered in American cities. This act required a tax to be paid for the official seals required on all newspapers and legal and commercial documents.

These taxes, added to hard economic times in the colonies, caused widespread anger. Sam Adams had used ruffians of the "South End mob," led by a waterfront thug named Ebenezer Mackintosh, to frighten those who tried to enforce the Stamp Act.

Mackintosh and his South End mob had smashed Stamp Tax headquarters. They hanged an effigy of Andrew Oliver, the Crown official in charge, on an oak known as the Liberty Tree. The mob then took down the effigy, carried it to Oliver's house, and there beheaded it. Some of the mob broke into the house, vowing to kill Oliver. He had fled in panic. Next day he resigned his office.

Adams had been delighted by this success. The day "ought to be forever remembered in America," he exulted, because "the People shouted; and their shout was heard to the distant end of this continent." The *Boston Gazette* noted, "The resistance of that day roused the spirit of America."

Mob rule reigned in Boston for three days. At Adams's instigation, another mob smashed into and looted the house of Lieutenant Governor Hutchinson, Oliver's brother-in-law. Adams was showing all the colonies that if they were bold enough, they could defy the king, Parliament, and all unjust tax laws.

Nine colonies took the cue. They organized a Stamp Act Congress that branded the act illegal—"taxation without consent"—and demanded its repeal. Parliament, worried about the rising anger against England in the colonies, yielded and repealed the Stamp Act.

The news brought great rejoicing in the colonies. Adams was at first thrilled with his victory but soon grew bored with the ensuing lack of public protest.

"The repeal of the Stamp Act," noted his cousin John Adams, "has hushed into silence almost every popular clamor and composed every wave of popular disorder into a smooth and peaceful calm."

"BOSTON HARBOR A TEAPOT TONIGHT!"

Parliamentary protest in England against removal of the stamp tax led the British to impose a new tariff—this one a tax on all tea imported into the colonies. At the same time the Tea Act gave a virtual tariff-free monopoly to the British East India Company. This meant higher prices for all other tea, which upset over a million colonists who drank tea at least twice daily.

"The women are such slaves to it," one Philadelphia paper observed, "that they would rather go without their dinners than without a dish of tea." Men in the colonies were no less devoted tea-drinkers.

Now Sam Adams had a new issue around which to arouse indignation and mob violence. He warned Americans that if they did not resist at every port where British tea was landed, they "would drink themselves out of their liberties."

Three British tea ships arrived in Boston harbor on December 16, 1773. Bostonians called a town meeting in Old South Church. Sam Adams assembled Mackintosh and his South End mob there. In speeches to the crowd, Adams and John Hancock demanded that Governor Hutchinson order the ships to take the tea back to England, and that he insist that Parliament rescind the tea tax.

Hutchinson refused. When his answer was conveyed to the jammed hall, Adams shouted, "Then this meeting can do nothing further to save the country." Hancock cried, "Let every man do what is right in his own eyes!"

That evening some 150 rioters disguised as Mohawk Indians and African captives followed Adams to the port. They swarmed aboard the tea ships. Crowds raced after them, joining in the rioting. They broke open 342 big chests of British tea. Howling in glee, the rioters dumped them into the harbor.

"Boston Harbor a teapot tonight!" Adams cried jubilantly.

From Boston to Dorchester, the ebbing tide smothered the sea in a surface of the fine tea that had been shipped to the colonies at great expense.

Parliament promptly punished the colonial rioters by passing the Boston Port Act. It shut down the harbor until Bostonians agreed to pay for the dumped tea. The new Quartering Act allowed the royal governor, General Thomas Gage, to take over private Boston homes for housing British soldiers.

Sam Adams at once labeled these acts, and three other punitive bills by Parliament, the "Intolerable Acts."

The colonial mobs that rioted between 1764 and 1774 did so primarily because the economic cost of submission to British rule had grown too oppressive. Taxation without consent became a burning issue. Sporadic riots of protest eventually united American resistance to such a level that the colonists finally felt compelled to fight for and win their freedom from Britain.

THE WHISKEY REBELLION

Many small farmers in remote areas of western Pennsylvania were not able to get their grain to market except by distilling it in the form of rye whiskey. These farmers were outraged when the secretary of the American treasury imposed a 25 percent tax on whiskey, amounting to nine cents a gallon.

The treasury secretary had had a threefold motive in imposing the whiskey tax. He wanted to raise money to reduce the government's national debt. He wanted to discourage excessive drinking. And he wanted to exert the federal government's power over states and regions.

The small farmers protested that the whiskey tax was just as unfair and tyrannical as Britain's tea tax had been. But the tea tax imposed on American colonists by the British had been taxation without representation, whereas the whiskey tax had been passed by an American government elected by the American people.

Nevertheless, when tax collectors and process servers began invading rural regions of Pennsylvania, New York, North Carolina, Virginia, and the Ohio Valley, violence erupted. Mobs of infuriated farmers drove the federal agents out. Rioters broke into, looted, and burned government officials' homes. They mobbed, tarred, and feathered farmers who submitted to paying the whiskey tax.

A Philadelphia court gave tax inspector John Neville orders for thirty-seven balky farmers in western Pennsylvania to appear in court. A frenzied mob of five hundred farmers led by James McFarlane drove him off. They then surged to Neville's house.

Finding he had fled, McFarlane gave the house's occupants, Neville's relatives and eleven soldiers, an ultimatum. "Surrender the house or surrender the subpoenas!" he thundered. "One or the other must be burned!"

The soldiers defied the mob. The rioters opened fire, which was returned. McFarlane was killed. Three soldiers and some rioters were wounded. The mob then forced those in the house to surrender, and they put the house to the torch.

Three weeks later a mob of ten thousand agitated farmers threatened to attack the courts in Pittsburgh. That city's officials hastily promised not to enforce the whiskey tax.

The date was July 1794. The secretary of the treasury who had imposed the burdensome whiskey tax on small farmers was Alexander Hamilton. He grew alarmed that the Whiskey Rebellion might spread into a united uprising.

"Shall the majority govern or be governed?" he demanded indignantly of President George Washington. The president then branded the attack on Neville's house an act of treason and ordered all rioters to disband. He warned, "The very existence of government and the fundamental principles of social order are materially involved." But the angry farmers persisted in their defiance. Hamilton pressed a reluctant Washington to raise a national army to crush the Whiskey Rebellion.

Washington agreed to a muster of militiamen from four states. Accordingly, Virginia Governor Henry Lee and Secretary Hamilton, who was ambitious for military glory, raised fifteen thousand troops. They led this force across the Allegheny Mountains. The mobs of farmers quickly melted away at the approach of the soldiers. The revolt collapsed.

"Take hold of all who are worth the trouble," Hamilton ordered his officers. He marched 150 captured farmers through Philadelphia at the point of bayonets. Trials of twenty found only two guilty of high treason. Washington pardoned both, one as a "simpleton," the other as "insane."

Hamilton's enemies criticized him bitterly for an excessive show of force. He insisted that lesser force would have permitted the riots to grow into full-scale insurrection.

" 'Tis better far to err on the other side," he maintained. "When the government appears in arms, it ought to appear like a Hercules, and inspire respect by the display of strength."

That same year, when Hamilton attempted to make a political speech from a balcony in New York's Wall Street, an angry mob roared him down and pelted him with stones. Blood streaming from his face, Hamilton told his opponents bitterly, "If you use such knockdown arguments, I must retire."

The Whiskey Rebellion had important political reverberations. Anti-Federalists who followed Thomas Jefferson accused Hamilton's Federalist party of an extreme overreaction to local riots. Hamilton had used the riots, they charged, as a pretext for establishing federal authority over the states. When the Jeffersonians came to power in 1801, they repealed the whiskey tax, and liquor went tax free for sixty years.

Because the economic costs had been too high for the small whiskey farmers, their rioting had precipitated the first clash between Hamiltonians, who believed in strong federal power, and Jeffersonians, who believed in strong states' rights.

FARMER RIOTS

More than a century later, farmers were once again in a desperate plight—not just those in one section of the country but those all over America. The Great Depression of the 1930s was leaving agriculture in a shambles. It ruined farm prices but did nothing to reduce taxes and mortgage obligations.

Thousands of farmers lost their land, unable to meet either taxes or bank payments. On a single day in April 1932 a quarter of all the farmland in Mississippi went under the hammer of auctioneers.

"Right here in Mississippi some people are about ready to lead a mob," growled Governor Theodore Bilbo. Then, indicating he considered demonstrations to be the work of "Red Communists," he added, "In fact, I'm getting a little pink myself!"

Grim-faced farmers formed armed mobs to keep each other's homesteads out of the hands of court officials and banks. Jamming into foreclosure auctions, they threatened to shoot any outsider who tried to bid for property put up on the auction block. Auctioneers were forced to sell property after bids of $1.00 and $1.18. The mob would then restore the property to its original owner.

"We will soon have no individually owned and operated farms," Iowa farm leader Milo Reno warned. "We have come to the place where you must practice what every other group does—strike!"

During the summer of 1932, Iowa farmers declared a "Farm Holiday" to stop food shipments into Sioux City until wholesalers paid farmers at least their cost of production. Mobs of farmers armed with ax handles blocked all the roads leading into Sioux City with logs and spiked telephone poles. When trucks sought to crash through the blockades, the mobs punctured their tires with pitchforks and smashed their windshields and headlights.

Police arrested fifty-five rioting farmers; a mob of a thousand more threatened to storm the jail, forcing their release on bail.

The Farm Holiday spread swiftly throughout Iowa. Farmers dumped thousands of gallons of milk into roadway ditches. They were seeking to dramatize the stupidity of an economic system that refused to pay farmers fair prices for their food, causing it to be wasted, while poor American families in the cities went hungry.

The governor of Iowa ordered all roads cleared. A mob of farmers descended upon a sheriff who tried to enforce the order. They took away his gun and badge, flinging them into a cornfield. Other sheriffs swore in carloads of deputies. They attempted to break through the blockades with truck convoys. But the mobs of farmers stood fast, guns raised and ready for battle. The deputies' trucks turned back.

Soon the Farm Holiday spread throughout the country. In Wisconsin dairy farmers also dumped milk on the road, and they fought stormy battles with deputy sheriffs. A Farm Holiday mob in Nebraska stopped a freight train headed for market and drove off a carload of cattle.

"If we don't get beneficial service from the Legislature," one mob leader warned, "two hundred thousand of us are coming to Lincoln [Nebraska's capital] and we'll tear that new state capitol building to pieces!"

Franklin D. Roosevelt, campaigning for the farm vote in Topeka, Kansas, in his bid for the presidency, told farmers, "We must have, I assert with all possible emphasis, national planning in agriculture."

He promised to ease farm credit to prevent mortgage foreclosures; to readjust tariffs to help overseas sales of surplus crops; and to compel local governments to cut farm taxes.

Once elected, Roosevelt invited the nation's farm organizations to come up with a program all could agree on. Secretary of Agriculture Henry Wallace consulted with them and helped develop a reform bill, the Agricultural Adjustment Act. But Congress balked at its passage.

Violence broke out once more in the Corn Belt. A mob of farmers masked in blue bandannas dragged Judge Charles C. Bradley from his bench in Le Mars, Iowa. They nearly lynched him before he promised not to sign any more mortgage foreclosures. The Farmers' Holiday Association called a national farmers' strike for May 1933.

Alarmed, Congress now hastily whipped through the administration's farm bill. Only then did the Farm Holiday mobs disband, and the farmers returned to their barns and fields.

The farmers had turned to violence when the economic cost of accepting a desperate situation became too high. But they did not win their objectives until after they had voted for a change of administration.

SEVEN

When Americans Clash over War

The president went to Congress to demand a declaration of war. He cited "the spectacle of injuries and indignities which have been heaped on our country." He won his declaration of war despite the fact that 38 percent of the House of Representatives and 41 percent of the Senate voted against it.

Many newspaper editorials had also voiced opposition to the war. Ultrapatriotic mobs supporting the president burst into the newspaper offices of many antiwar editors, driving them out of town and smashing their presses. In Baltimore one mob wheeled a cannon in front of an editor's house. The editor's defenders within opened fire, killing and wounding some attackers.

The enraged mob stormed the house. Those within were saved from the wrath of the mob only by the arrival of troops. The soldiers spirited the editor and his defenders off to jail for their own protection.

But the mob thundered after them, smashing into the jail. One general who tried to stop the rioters was killed and another was battered so savagely that he could neither talk nor eat solid food for two months. The mob seized and tortured their prisoners and beat them insensible.

The year was 1812. President James Madison had declared war against the British. He accused them of seizing American sailors on the high seas and forcing them to serve on British ships; of violating U.S. shipping rights; and of blockading U.S. ports. Americans opposed to the war argued that France was doing much the same as Britain. They accused Madison of letting himself be used as a pawn by the French against the British.

The mobs that rioted were intent upon silencing those opposed to the war. The general who had been seriously injured trying to stop the rioters in Baltimore was General Henry Lee, father of Robert E. Lee.

Ironically, the antiwar protesters were proved right in their opposition. It was learned later that Britain had agreed to redress Madison's grievances *before* his declaration of war. But because of the slowness of communication in those days, this information did not reach the president until the war had begun.

In this instance mob violence helped a president win support for a war that later proved to have been unnecessary.

"NO DRAFT! NO DRAFT!"

Government marshals were uneasy as they turned the wheel of the draft lottery in New York City. They were aware that a mob of about a thousand angry workers had gathered outside.

Suddenly a pistol shot was fired into the draft office. Then stones came hurtling through the windows in an electrifying crash.

The mob swept some police aside and surged against the doors, bursting them open. Shouting and yelling, they swarmed over the building, smashing furniture and chasing draft officials. They splintered the lottery wheel and tore up all draft records, scattering the pieces. Then they set the building on fire, cheering as flames crackled into the sky.

Some rioters caught sight of Police Superintendent John A. Kennedy hurrying to the turbulent scene.

"There's Kennedy! Get him!"

The mob closed in. Blows rained down, shoving Kennedy into a vacant lot. He tried to flee, only to be set upon by a second mob that caught him near a wide mud hole.

"Drown him! Drown him!" A heavy blow from a club sent the chief of New York's police headlong into the mud. The mob trampled and kicked him savagely before he could escape.

The rioters fought off police who sought to arrest them. They surged through the city, armed with clubs, rocks, knives, and guns. Thousands of other draft protesters poured out of factories and shipyards to join them.

"No draft!" they roared. *"No draft!"*

Other mobs surged through other neighborhoods. New York City took on the appearance of a city in revolution.

The date was July 13, 1863. The Civil War's bloody Battle of Gettysburg had inflicted twenty-three thousand Union casualties. President Abraham Lincoln had put a new draft call into action to replace them.

Most laborers in New York City who were subject to the draft were poor Americans of Irish descent. They were enraged because wealthy Americans subject to the draft were allowed to get out of serving in the army by paying three hundred dollars—a large sum in those days—to hire substitutes to take their places. The laborers were also bitter at being compelled to join in "a rich man's war and a poor man's fight."

Many laborers also resented fighting a civil war to benefit blacks held in slavery—especially when free blacks in the North were being hired as strikebreakers against white waterfront unions.

One mob surged to attack publisher-editor Horace Greeley's *Tribune*, which championed the abolitionist cause and the war.

"Burn the *Tribune!*" they roared. "Hang old Greeley!"

They stormed the building and began smashing its presses. Army troops drove them out.

As night fell, white rioters began hunting the scapegoats they blamed for the war and the draft—free black Americans. They seized and beat one man severely, then hanged him from a tree. Frightened blacks sought refuge from the mobs in police stations.

Meanwhile the flames consuming draft headquarters spread to other buildings. A mob of fifty thousand watched and cheered. Some clamored for the burning of every factory that employed blacks. A small body of troops fired a warning volley over the mob's heads. Infuriated rioters fell upon the soldiers, snatching their muskets and clubbing the troops into flight. They beat some soldiers senseless and left them in the street for dead.

Police squads counterattacked. But they found themselves drowning in a swarm of bodies. Iron bars, clubs, and bricks smashed against their faces. Those police who could do so escaped, battered and bleeding. Some were knocked unconscious or killed, then stripped and robbed. A woman wielding a shoemaker's knife led one mob chasing an officer.

Fire companies sought to fight the blazing buildings. The mobs drove them off until a fire chief assured the rioters that draft headquarters had been totally destroyed.

Tuesday morning, July 14, dawned on a city stupefied by shock. Stores and factories stayed closed as an early mob of ten thousand poured into the streets. Police and seven hundred troops marched to break up the mob. At their approach many rioters ran to the rooftops, hurling down rocks and brickbats.

Fifty policemen ran after them. One rioter they clubbed fell off the roof, plunging to his death. Police beat others insensible, dragged them down the stairs, then threw them into the street. Troops brought up two howitzers and trained them on the mob. The rioters charged, shouting defiance. The howitzers fired point-blank. The soldiers' muskets roared.

Men and women fell, shrieking in agony. One woman was killed with a baby in her arms. The mob scattered in panic.

Other mobs roamed the city, seeking revenge. Rioters and police fought savagely, filling the pavements and gutters with bleeding and dying people. Clanging fire bells told of new buildings going up in flames. Shouts and cries from every direction signaled chaotic street fighting.

"AS HOUNDS WOULD CHASE A FOX"

Mobs continued to hunt down blacks savagely—"as hounds would chase a fox," Major Edward Sanford wired Secretary of War Henry Stanton. One mob that killed a black man stripped him and did a triumphant dance around his body. Mobs chased blacks who dared venture onto the streets. Many had to dive into the river to save their lives.

Toward evening reinforced troops and police took the offensive. One large mob threw up street barricades made by lashing together carts and wagons. They erected four such barricades, one behind the other. As soldiers opened fire, police braved a hail of flying rocks to tear down the barricades.

The mob fell back behind each rear barricade in turn. Intense troop fire at last forced the rioters to flee in wild disorder, leaving behind forty dead and wounded.

On the third day of the riots an armed mob again battled troops, this time forcing them to retreat. Black bodies now hung from lamp-posts all over the city. Troops attempting to cut them down were attacked. They in turn fired canisters and grapeshot point-blank into charging mobs. Often they had to fire five or six rounds before the rioters were driven off. Street battles raged in every quarter of the city.

Rioters continued to gut, loot, and set fire to stores. Governor

Horatio Seymour finally declared the city to be in a state of insurrection.

By the fourth day, Thursday, July 16, President Lincoln felt compelled to withdraw major Union troops from Gettysburg and send them to New York to restore order. If he allowed the rioters to defeat the draft in New York, it would mean the end of the draft in every northern city—and the end of the war.

Mayor George Opdyke called on New Yorkers to form street patrols to protect their districts from the roving mobs. In the hope of dividing the ranks of rioters, he announced that the draft had been suspended for the time being. And he promised that three hundred dollars in exemption money would be paid to any poor citizen who might be drafted, to give him the chance to also pay for a substitute.

These concessions might have prevented the riots in the first place. But by this time, mob passions had soared too high, and too much blood had been spilled. Mobs continued to overflow the streets, angrily vowing vengeance against the military and police for "conducting warfare against the people."

One large mob assailed a platoon of soldiers and forced them to take refuge in a factory. Troop reinforcements rescued them by routing the rioters with fixed bayonets. The mob took out their fury by smashing and looting stores in every direction. When troops pursued them, hundreds of rioters raced up to the rooftops and poured down a murderous musketfire.

Troops rushed in with howitzers and swept the streets with canister shot. Wounded bodies lay thick upon the pavement. The troops then stormed the buildings, fighting pitched battles in narrow halls, on staircases, and on roofs. Many rioters fought desperately until they were killed. The survivors fled.

Bringing up cannons, the Union troops from Gettysburg finally restored an uneasy peace on the fifth day of the tumult.

The riots had caused more deaths in those five days of anarchy than all the riots in the nation did a century later, during the violent

1960s. There were at least fifteen hundred known dead. The actual figure was higher because of many unreported burials. An undetermined number of lynching victims had also been cut down and thrown in the river.

Over three thousand blacks were left homeless. One out of five black New Yorkers chose to move to more law-abiding cities. After the riots, not a single black worker showed up on New York's docks.

Other, less bloody draft riots erupted in Newark, Jersey City, Troy, Boston, Toledo, and Evansville. The riots finally forced changes in the draft laws to eliminate discrimination against the poor. During the Civil War 255,000 northerners were drafted. Significantly, of this number 204,000 were substitutes, paid for by those who avoided serving.

ATTACKS AGAINST PROTESTERS

When the president declared war after promising that he would not do so, opponents of the war protested vehemently. Superpatriot vigilante mobs attacked and silenced them.

Pacifist minister Herbert Bigelow spoke out against the war in Newport, Kentucky. A mob seized, bound, and gagged him. They drove him into a forest and lashed him unconscious with a blacksnake whip. The U.S. Attorney General's office refused to investigate because charges had not been brought by a "responsible citizen."

Vigilante mobs punished workers who dared strike—said to "interfere" with the war effort—with beatings, kidnappings, lynchings, and mass deportations out of town, county, and state.

In Bisbee, Arizona, a mob of two thousand businessmen and mining officials had themselves made deputies. Then they rounded up 1,284 strikers and forced them into cattle-train boxcars, sealing the doors. They sent the train into the blazing New Mexico desert and dumped the strikers there, leaving them to their own resources without food or water.

In Oklahoma poor tenant farmers and sharecroppers tried to march to Washington to protest the war. Vigilante mobs attacked and dispersed them. Oklahoma Home Guards arrested not the vigilantes but over 450 farmers for "conspiracy to oppose the draft." A court sentenced some to jail for ten years.

The war was World War I, declared by President Woodrow Wilson in 1917. Wilson saw to it that Socialist leader Eugene Debs was sentenced to ten years for opposing the war and that Debs was stripped of his citizenship. "This man was a traitor to his country!" Wilson insisted. Debs's crime had been to insist that the war was an imperialistic conflict over world markets.

This view contradicted Wilson's assertion that the war was a "crusade to save the world for democracy." Yet in 1920, after the war, Wilson addressed a crowd in St. Louis and admitted that Debs, the man he had jailed, had been right.

"Who does not know that the seed of war in the modern world is industrial and commercial rivalry?" he asked then. "The real reason that the war . . . took place was that Germany was afraid her commercial rivals were going to get the better of her and . . . they thought Germany would get the commercial advantage of them."

Yet the United States government had encouraged superpatriot mobs to take violent action against those who had opposed an unnecessary, cynical war that cost over fifty-three thousand American lives.

"NO MILITARY ON CAMPUS!"

In 1970 the Vietnam War was still going on, despite increasingly outraged protests. The uproar had forced President Lyndon B. Johnson to forgo seeking a second term. Richard M. Nixon had won the 1968 election with the promise that he had a secret plan to end the unpopular war.

Instead, Nixon expanded the war by ordering the invasion of Cambodia. College students across the country saw his decision as a betrayal of his campaign promise. Nixon further inflamed them by labeling militant antiwar protesters "campus bums."

A furious mob of four hundred students from Kent State University in Ohio built a protest bonfire in the town of Kent. They began smashing the windows of various businesses to express their resentment of the "Establishment," which they blamed for the war. Some of the student mob burned down the ROTC building on campus. Mayor Leroy Satrom proclaimed a state of civil emergency and asked Ohio Governor James Rhodes for national guardsmen. Rhodes dispatched some one hundred helmeted, gas-masked guardsmen to Kent.

The guardsmen moved onto the campus with loaded rifles. At noon on May 4, 1970, over twelve hundred students gathered on the commons to protest both the invasion of Cambodia and the presence of the guardsmen. The officer leading the guardsmen ordered the students to disperse, calling them an "unlawful mob."

"Pigs off campus!" the students cried defiantly.

The guardsmen fired tear gas from grenade launchers, forcing the gasping, choking, weeping students back. Scattering, the students shouted bitterly, "Toy soldiers! Murderers! Weekend warriors! Fascists!"

The guardsmen advanced upon the retreating students with fixed bayonets. From a distance a few students continued to shout taunts and hurl rocks ineffectively.

In a scene eerily reminiscent of the Boston Massacre, the guardsmen suddenly opened fire without an order and without giving any warning. They shot fifteen students, who crumpled to the ground. Four of these—two men and two women—were killed.

A horrified student slipped to her knees beside one dead boy's body and screamed in terror. "I saw the men firing, and I saw the kids fall," Lucia Perry, 18, later recalled, "and I looked out at the crowd and there were people . . . with blood all over them down the hill, and I just couldn't believe it. I've never seen people so mad and so horrified.... There's no way to describe the pain that I saw in people's faces."

The president of Kent State forbade outraged students and faculty from gathering on campus to mourn the fallen students.

"What really struck me," one professor said afterward, "was that my rights were taken away, just like that. I saw how tenuous our rights really are, even in this so-called democratic country. If you can't have your freedom of assembly, your freedom of speech is curtailed."

UNIVERSITIES PROTEST
THE KENT STATE MURDERS

Within a few days hundreds of colleges and universities were shut down by a faculty-supported student strike to protest both the Kent State killings and the Cambodia invasion. One week later an extension of the strike had closed twenty-five hundred institutions of higher learning—the first sustained national student strike in U.S. history.

The Kent State killings sparked an angry debate. Who had actually been at fault—the student demonstrators or the National Guard who had shot them? An ultraconservative county grand jury exonerated the guardsmen on grounds that the troops' lives had been endangered by the student rioting. The grand jury then indicted students and faculty members identified as having been involved in the antiwar demonstration.

Senator Stephen M. Young of Ohio accused the guardsmen of having been "trigger-happy." He insisted that the four dead students had been brutally murdered. An investigation found that seven of the injured students had bullets in their sides and backs, proving they were not advancing on but fleeing from the guardsmen.

Newspaper reporters also learned that none of the four dead victims had been involved in the demonstration in any way. The guardsmen had lied when they claimed to have been fired upon by a sniper.

Some guardsmen had aimed deliberately at students, while others had fired in panic.

It was clear that no guardsman had been in any real danger. Nevertheless, Nixon's attorney general, John Mitchell, refused to convene a federal grand jury. He insisted there was no evidence requiring an FBI investigation.

Two years later a new attorney general, Elliot Richardson, decreed that county grand jury hearings had been a whitewash of the guardsmen. He then ordered the indictment of the guardsmen who had shot at the students.

One guardsman revealed, "The guys have been saying that we got to get together and stick to the same story, that it was our lives or them, a matter of survival. I told them I would tell the truth." The truth, he explained, was that the four dead students had been killed as a result of mob psychology in the guardsmen's own ranks: "It was an automatic thing. Everybody shot, so I shot. I didn't think about it. I just fired. . . ."

A subsequent report found that eight of the guardsmen had intended to shoot. These were the men indicted by Elliott Richardson.

As in the Chicago police riot at the 1968 Democratic Convention, most Americans at the time were upset by antiwar demonstrators but not at the government's use of violence in Vietnam and against demonstrators at home. A Gallup poll survey showed that 58 percent of the public blamed the demonstrating students, not the National Guard, for the Kent State killings.

"GET THE TRAITORS!"

Four days after the Kent State murders, Mayor John Lindsay of New York lowered the flag at City Hall to half-mast in honor of the dead students. Students organized an antiwar demonstration on Wall Street.

A mob of a thousand hard-hat construction workers, supporters of President Nixon and the Vietnam War, invaded City Hall to demand that Mayor Lindsay raise the flag. They carried signs reading: GET THE HIPPIES! GET THE TRAITORS! Racing to Wall Street, they broke up the student demonstration. The hard-hats attacked every long-haired youth within sight, injuring nearly seventy with fists and clubs. Police turned their backs.

One worker expressed his resentment of student demonstrators: "We put our sweat and blood into building this city. Now these punks want to bring it all down with bombs and riots. They ain't American. Send 'em to Russia. This is our city and our country. We built it!"

President Nixon invited Peter Brennan, head of the construction workers' union, to the White House. Brennan presented the president with a hard hat and pinned an American flag on his lapel. The president thus made it clear that he favored letting mob violence suppress antiwar demonstrations.

Republican Senator Jacob Javits observed that "an insidious form of repression" of dissent was being "tolerated, if not actually condoned, at the highest level of our government." Federal Communications Commissioner Nicholas Johnson warned that by "bottling up legitimate means for communication of dissent," the administration would "leave only the avenues of violence and despair."

Mob violence opposing the Civil War draft had succeeded in compelling the government to change the law that discriminated against the poor and favored the rich. The rioters felt that they had no alternative but to exhibit their rage by mob violence. It worked, whereas their peaceful protests had previously been ignored.

In the 1970s police and soldiers had rioted against students demonstrating against the Vietnam War at Kent State and shot four of them. And police had looked the other way in New York when hard-hats beat student antiwar demonstrators.

A subsequent poll revealed that prior to the use of police against students, 90 percent of students had held a favorable opinion of police.

Police rioting or indifference now led 90 percent of students to consider them brutal and unfair.

In 1971 a Gallup poll asked Americans to name the country's biggest problem. Most Americans cited the seething unrest on college campuses. But instead of listening to student protests, government and university authorities chose to ignore them. When student frustration erupted in demonstrations and riots at Kent State, authorities responded by using deadly force to suppress them.

There will always be protests against war—almost certainly against wars of aggression, when a nation's own safety is not at stake. Attempts to ignore or choke off peaceful protest can be expected to result in violence.

When Despair Breeds Violence

Panic swept white southerners when they believed that the whole population of enslaved blacks had risen in rebellion. They had long feared that the African-Americans they held in bondage would, out of despair over their bleak lives, revolt in a bloody uprising against them.

The rebellion began in August 1831 with 31-year-old Nat Turner, held in slavery in Virginia. He fasted, preached, read the Bible, heard voices, and told his revelations to his people. He had heard "a loud noise in the heavens," and a spirit had appeared to reveal that Turner had been chosen by God to lead the enslaved Africans out of bondage.

Turner and five others killed their sleeping master, his wife, and the couple's three children. Seizing guns and ammunition, they sped from plantation to plantation gathering recruits, until they had assembled a mob of seventy men. In each house they burst into, the mob assassinated all white occupants and seized muskets, axes, scythes, clubs, and swords. They smashed property and stole money and horses. In two days they killed over fifty-seven white men, women, and children in a twenty-mile area.

The alarm flashed around the countryside, then all through the

South. Militia units, three companies of artillery, and detachments of men from two offshore warships joined forces to suppress the Turner mob. They swept through Virginia and killed over one hundred blacks indiscriminately. Many were captured and massacred on the spot. Some were beheaded.

Nineteen people were tried and executed. Turner, captured after two months, was hanged. William Lloyd Garrison defended the rioting mob in his newspaper. They were no more guilty, he insisted, than "the Greeks in destroying the Turks, or the Poles in exterminating the Russians, or our fathers in slaughtering the British."

Subsequently, many southern states passed even more repressive measures against blacks held in slavery. Some states set a 10:00 P.M. curfew. In South Carolina, the circulation of any publication inciting enslaved blacks to riot was punishable by death. One mob of angry Charleston citizens broke into the post office, seized packages of antislavery pamphlets from the mail, and burned them. Alabama passed a law forbidding anyone to teach any enslaved black person to read, write, or spell, under penalty of a five-hundred-dollar fine.

These riots brought about harsh repressive measures against all those who were held in bondage. But their violent protests against their condition gradually won recruits to the abolitionist cause.

AFTER THE CIVIL WAR

A coalition of southern blacks and northern whites sought control of the government in Louisiana, hoping to take over the state capitol in New Orleans. A crowd of black men marched jubilantly down Canal Street behind a small brass band led by a flag bearer.

A sullen white mob gathered in the baking streets. One white boy ran alongside the black marchers, jeering and taunting them. A marcher lost his temper and fired a pistol into the air to frighten the boy off.

That shot provided the spark the New Orleans police and the

white mob had been waiting for. Police opened fire on the marchers. A mob of over two thousand charged the procession, driving it off with a hail of bricks and stones.

A second white mob attacked the Mechanics Institute Hall, where union members were seeking to establish suffrage for blacks. The mob fired shots at some unionists watching the riot from windows. The unionists fell to the floor as bullets shattered the glass over them. Rioters led by police burst into the hall. They fired wildly at the figures lying on the floor. Blacks leapt out of the smashed windows, only to be shot down or stabbed by police outside.

"Police came up to Negroes and white men, indiscriminately taking no prisoners, but shooting them as rapidly as possible," State Senator J. D. O'Connell testified later at a Congressional hearing. "I saw one policeman, while a Negro was kneeling before him and begging for mercy, shoot into his side. I saw another discharge his revolver into a Negro lying flat on the floor. . . . I saw a line of police [outside] . . . fire their revolvers into the hall."

By the time federal troops arrived to control the rampaging mob, at least thirty-eight people had been killed, and a hundred and forty-six had been wounded. "It was not just a riot but an absolute massacre by the police," reported General Phil Sheridan, ". . . a murder which the mayor and police perpetrated without the shadow of necessity."

The date was July 30, 1866. At the close of the Civil War, the white ruling class in the South had desperately sought to retain power. They barred blacks from voting and passed "Black Codes" to keep former slaves in bondage.

"We hold this to be a Government of the White People," decreed the Democrats in Louisiana, "made and to be perpetuated for the exclusive benefit of the White Race."

But the "carpetbaggers" (white migrants from the North) and "scalawags" (southern white Republicans) were determined to outlaw the Black Codes, strip ex-Confederates of their vote, and give it instead to black freedmen.

The federal government put the southern states under its control as part of the process of Reconstruction. The Republican-controlled Congress included southern blacks as officials of the new ruling state governments south of the Mason-Dixon line.

Southern whites were frightened and despairing. They had lost the Civil War, and the South lay in ruins. They regarded the new carpetbagger state governments as federal tyranny imposed upon them. Most were in deadly fear of revenge from northern whites for the Civil War and from blacks for having been kept in slavery. They saw no other way to stave off disaster but by waging mob attacks on the carpetbagger regimes, hoping to drive them out of the South.

The New Orleans riot gave the Republican-controlled Congress an excuse for branding the whole South as "unregenerate," undeserving of self-government. In fall elections the Republicans captured two-thirds of the seats in Congress. That gave them the power to keep the South under federal bayonets.

Eight years after the New Orleans riot another mob attempted to drive out the carpetbagger state government. A pitched battle with federal troops in the streets of New Orleans left twenty-seven dead and over a hundred wounded.

In the South election-day riots have often stemmed from a white mob's efforts to keep blacks from voting. This repression became a major cause of the civil rights campaigns of the 1960s, an era that provoked violent mob resistance by many white southerners.

VETERANS MARCH ON WASHINGTON

Despair brought over twenty thousand jobless war veterans into Washington from every direction. Thousands of firms were bankrupt, factories were closed, long breadlines had formed in cities all across the country, and college graduates were selling apples on street corners to make some income. The desperate veterans descended on the nation's capital; they demanded the military bonus that Congress had promised them to be paid after the war, to compensate for their sacrifice in leaving jobs to fight overseas for their country. But the bonus bill had been frozen in a congressional committee.

The penniless veterans hitchhiked to Washington from every state. Unable to pay for tickets, many caught freight trains. A ragged mob, they were dressed in frayed pants, jackets, and shirts, faded jeans, and torn sweaters. Hostile stationmasters and railroad deputies threw many veterans off the freight trains as "bums."

At the Baltimore & Ohio railroad yards in East St. Louis, 150 railroad police wearing deputy badges wielded clubs to force 300 veterans off one freight train. The veterans refused to budge. A mass battle threatened. Newspaper headlines read: "Bonus Army Clash Stirs Nation. . . . Capital Girds for Invasion."

East St. Louis police tried to arrest some veterans they singled out as leaders. But all three hundred veterans insisted that the police had to lock them *all* up and feed them in jail. The police tried to get the B & O Railroad to let the veterans continue riding the freight out of Illinois, but the railroad refused. The perplexed police chief phoned Governor Louis Lincoln Emmerson.

"I don't care how you do it," the governor roared, "but get those . . . veterans out of Illinois! If the B & O won't let them ride, get them into Indiana somehow—I don't care how. Let Indiana worry about them!"

A cavalcade of fifty trucks, sedans, and dump carts rumbled into the freight yard. The veterans agreed to transfer to them and continue on into Indiana. Newspaper headlines reported: "Battle of E. St. Louis Ends . . . Bonus Marchers Win Transportation . . . Vets Everywhere Joining March on Washington."

Thousands of veterans arrived in Washington by freight train or jalopy; others hitchhiked or came on foot. Many brought their wives and children. Some carried signs reading: BONUS ARMY . . . GIVE US OUR BONUS—OR JOBS.

It was June 1932, at the height of the depression. President Herbert

Hoover continued to promise Americans that "prosperity [was] just around the corner." But when the number of unemployed grew to over fifteen million, a roar of discontent swept the country. Hoover actually feared that the thousands of veterans descending on Washington might, in their anger, attempt to overthrow the government.

One group of veterans sought to move into an old, half-demolished office building. Police shoved away men carrying bundles and packs. The veterans fought back.

A sympathetic Washington, D.C., superintendent of police, Pelham Glassford, was a veteran himself. He stopped the fighting by ordering police to let the veterans move into the empty building.

The veterans demanded that the House Ways and Means Committee unfreeze the bonus bill and let the full House vote on it. The committee chairman refused. He pointed out that the president opposed the bill and would veto it if it passed Congress.

The Bonus Army swelled to over twenty thousand. Police Superintendent Glassford permitted newly arriving veterans to move into empty stores, abandoned buildings, and some vacant lots.

Soon he had run out of places in the city to put veterans and their families. He bivouacked thousands of new arrivals into a camp at Anacostia Flats on the outskirts of Washington. He tried to persuade Washington officials that by helping the veterans he was keeping them under control and preventing rioting.

THE PRESIDENT WANTS THEM OUT

But President Hoover, a Republican, was exasperated. He wanted the twenty thousand ragged veterans out of Washington, to avoid personal embarrassment when the Republican Convention met that month in Chicago.

About ten thousand veterans and their families roosting at Anacostia Flats put up signs reading: HOOVER'S POOR FARM. They erected tar-paper shacks and used egg crates and tarpaulin lean-tos as shelters against the rain.

The House of Representatives grew alarmed by the presence of the rapidly swelling Bonus Army in Washington. The representatives hastily passed the bonus bill. Crowds of veterans gathered outside the Capitol, shouting demands that the Senate likewise pass the bill.

The Senate voted against it. Outraged cries rose among the veterans. Some called for rushing inside the Capitol and tearing the Senate to pieces. Nervous Capitol police positioned themselves on the steps, batons at the ready.

Congress sought to avoid violence by voting for funds for train tickets to persuade the veterans to return home. Many agreed to leave. Bitter fights broke out between the veterans lining up for railroad tickets and those determined to stay. Twenty were injured.

California veterans formed a "death watch" in front of the Capitol. "It's going on day and night until we drop dead," one veteran vowed to reporters, "or get the bonus. Whichever comes first." A *New York Times* headline read: "Death March Upsets Hoover."

When veterans learned that Congress was preparing to adjourn, a mob of them marched on the Capitol, carrying signs: CONGRESS MUST NOT ADJOURN! . . . WE DECIDED WHEN TO COME—WE'LL DECIDE WHEN TO GO . . . DO WE STARVE WHILE CONGRESS TAKES A VACATION? Veterans' children carried signs reading: I'M HELPING DADDY GET THE BONUS.

A cordon of police tried to block the veterans from access to the Capitol steps. Mob pressure forced them back. The veterans covered the plaza and lower steps, then sat down. Alarmed congressmen left the House and Senate through the Congressional tunnel. Learning they had gone, the furious mob decided to march on the White House and demand to see the president.

President Hoover ordered the White House guard doubled. A motorcycle patrol cleared the area for two blocks around. White House guards armed with nightsticks and tear gas confronted and attacked the marchers, routing them.

General George Van Horn Moseley told the president, "Intelligence is convinced that a veterans' riot will be the signal for a Communist uprising in all large cities. Revolution!"

Hoover nodded. "We must begin to be firm. The veterans must now be forced out of Washington as quickly as possible!" He issued orders to compel all veterans occupying buildings in Washington to evacuate them within twenty-four hours or they would face arrest and sentences of up to six months in jail for vagrancy.

A mob of veterans again marched on the White House, to protest this order. They were stopped by police swinging clubs, and a melee began. The fighting spread over the street, engulfing passersby, who were attacked by the police indiscriminately. Many veterans were arrested.

Next morning Hoover officials sent a huge crane with a wrecking ball to knock down a partly demolished building on Pennsylvania Avenue occupied by veterans and their families. Hundreds of veterans rushed to stop the wreckers. Some seventy policemen surrounded the crane and pressed the veterans back. They ordered all veterans to vacate the buildings or face arrest.

Treasury agents backed up by police forced the veterans out.

The news flashed to Anacostia Flats. Thousands of enraged veterans rushed to the aid of their comrades. They came in old jalopies and beat-up trucks, carrying improvised clubs. Defying the swinging nightsticks, they charged the police lines. In the battle that raged, some went down on both sides. The veterans hurled a hail of bricks, rocks, and scrap iron, forcing the police to retreat.

One policeman fired his gun three times, killing a veteran. Furious veterans rushed to attack the officer. He began firing wildly all around him. Another officer also began shooting, killing a second veteran. Four police were injured seriously enough to require hospitalization.

PRESIDENT HOOVER ORDERS
THE ARMY TO ATTACK

General Douglas MacArthur now told the president, "General Moseley believes the time has come to force them out of Washington with troops, even if it means some bloodshed."

Under White House orders, Navy Admiral Henry V. Butler dispatched sixty Marines to attack and disperse veteran mobs.

At the Fort Myers cavalry field, General George Patton trained troops to move through tear gas with gas masks and fixed bayonets. "If tear gas fails to move a mob, open fire," he instructed. "Shoot into the rear ranks, selecting apparent leaders. Always fire to kill. If a few casualties become martyrs, a large number learn an object lesson. Use the bayonet to encourage retreat."

At a press conference President Hoover declared: "In order to put an end to this rioting and defiance of civil authority, I have asked the Army to assist the District authorities in restoring order."

MacArthur deployed a machine-gun company near the Capitol grounds. Then he ordered out a battalion of infantry, a squadron of cavalry, and a platoon of tanks. He declared he would lead these troops against the veterans himself.

"The Army will move down Pennsylvania Avenue, sweeping through the billets there, then cleaning out Camp Anacostia," he said. "It will be one continuous operation. When it finishes tonight, the B.E.F. [Bonus Expeditionary Force] will no longer be in Washington."

He directed the assault on the veterans from an army staff car. Colonel Dwight D. Eisenhower rode at his side. Cavalry units led by General Patton preceded them. The cavalrymen wore slung carbines and brandished sabers. They also wore steel helmets and carried gas masks and tear-gas bombs.

Behind the staff car came the infantry, in four columns of thirty men abreast. They also carried gas masks, and they held rifles with bayonets fixed in attack positions. They were followed by six army tanks, several 2½-ton open army trucks with manned machine guns, and more infantry.

Spectators and shoppers with baby carriages watched in amazement as this deadly war mobilization marched down Pennsylvania Avenue. "It was an incredible spectacle," one reporter wrote. "Peacetime American soldiers who had never been in battle declaring war on American soldiers who had fought for the country in World War I."

The cavalry halted at the building where the riot had taken place earlier in the day. Troops began chasing veterans and their families out of the building. The veterans fought back with a volley of bricks and rocks. The troops donned gas masks and hurled tear-gas bombs into the building as they advanced.

One bomb fell in an adjacent yard, causing two small African-American girls to fall to the ground, choking and screaming. Gasping women rushed out of the building, carrying crying children. Some spectators yelled, "Shame! Shame!"

Cavalrymen rode up on the sidewalks, swinging their sabers. "Clear out!" they roared. "Clear out!"

Spectators tumbled all over each other in their panic to escape the horses and sabers. Excited cavalrymen jabbed, slashed, and whacked with their sabers to force the mobs back. Infantrymen followed, prodding people with their bayonets and hurling tear-gas bombs.

Eight small children lay in the doorway of a five-and-dime store, agonized by exposure to the gas. Weeping mothers put wet cloths over their children's eyes to relieve their pain. Many veterans fled from the choking tear gas as the infantrymen routed them with bayonets. Cavalrymen scattered others by hitting them with the flat sides of their sabers.

Infantrymen set fire to shacks constructed between the semi-demolished buildings. Sobbing women and children stood apart with veteran husbands, clutching pots and pans and a few household belongings.

The troops continued their advance beyond the burning shacks. They cleared one semidemolished building at a time, chasing forty to one hundred veterans out of each one with bayonets and tear gas. Police clubbed those who were hurling bricks.

A few veterans dodged the swirling cavalry sabers and grabbed two horses' reins, twisting them around. Onlookers cheered when they pulled the two cavalrymen out of their saddles. Enraged cavalrymen charged into the veterans, trampling them. Some people fell into excavations while trying to avoid the rearing hooves and swirling sabers.

Now rioting out of control, the cavalrymen attacked veterans and civilians indiscriminately. They rode their horses up onto the sidewalks. Reporters and photographers scrambled into automobiles to escape being trampled.

Inch by inch, foot by foot, the troops forced hundreds of veterans back down Pennsylvania Avenue, herding them toward the river and Anacostia Bridge. They marched over veterans and bystanders who had been knocked down or who had fallen in the press of the mobs.

One veteran hurled a brick that hit General Patton, knocking him off his horse. Remounting, Patton ordered cavalrymen to wheel their horses and gallop headlong into the veterans, bowling them over.

THE ARMY DRIVES THE VETERANS OUT

The cavalry cleared a path ahead to Anacostia Bridge by tossing teargas bombs. Some fleeing veterans picked up the bombs and hurled them back. A weeping woman on her knees, choking and coughing, tried to resuscitate her dead baby in a blue haze of gas.

In the evening MacArthur's forces marched across Anacostia Bridge to clear the shacks and tents from the flats. Over four hundred children and seven hundred women were still in the encampment. Hearing the troops advance, the women grabbed their children and what possessions they could carry and hurried to the farthest reaches of the camp. The infantry surged forward, wearing gas masks and hurling tear-gas bombs.

Hundreds of veterans who had been in the camp, or who were forced back into it, scattered with their families, retreating to the south. Some of those in jalopies, unable either to turn or back up, abandoned their vehicles. They ran from the tear gas and advancing bayonets. Women fled screaming, some dragging or carrying their crying children. The soldiers set fire to the shacks with torches. The sky glowed with the orange haze of burning huts and tents.

A mob of about a thousand veterans attacked troops and cavalry with stones and hurled objects. The cavalry charged into them, bowling over veterans and their wives like tenpins. Some veterans tried to drag a cavalry captain off his mount but were driven away by infantry bayonets. Some fell with bayonet and saber wounds.

Tanks clattered through the fires and ruins of the camp, crushing unburned shacks. A group of veterans carrying a white flag of truce approached a line of advancing troops. The soldiers pitched tear gas at them, forcing them to retreat. One soldier raced after a veteran and speared him in the backside. The man fell, rolling on the ground in agony.

One group of veterans and their wives locked arms and faced the cavalry. They defiantly sang "My Country 'Tis of Thee." The captain of the cavalry hesitated a moment, then led a charge against them. The singers broke ranks and ran from the swinging sabers. The women screamed in fright.

Ambulances raced through the fires, horns blasting. The remaining veterans ran southeast to escape the troops. The last huts at Anacostia went up in flames.

Secretary of War Pat Hurley later told reporters: "At Anacostia there was an attack by several thousand men entirely controlled by

Red agitators whose sole purpose was to bring about disorder, riots, bloodshed, and death. . . . It is grossly untrue that the troops set fire to the shacks in Anacostia Flats to keep the veterans from returning."

A radio broadcaster summed up the rout of the Bonus Army: "Among the results achieved by the Hoover Administration's war on the Bonus Army are these. Two veterans of the World War shot to death. One 11-week-old baby dead of tear gas, shock, and exposure. One 8-year-old boy partially blinded by gas. One 7-year-old boy bayoneted in the leg. One veteran's ear severed with a cavalry saber. One veteran slashed in the hip by a saber. Over a dozen veterans stabbed with bayonets. Sixty people treated for injuries. Over a thousand men, women, and children gassed, including policemen, reporters, ambulance drivers, and residents of Washington."

A storm of telegrams flooded the White House. Over 90 percent condemned the administration's handling of the Bonus Army. The nation's press accused both Hoover and MacArthur of callous brutality toward jobless veterans who once had been hailed as patriotic heroes.

Veterans across the country vowed to vote President Hoover out of office in the elections of 1932. The general population joined them in defeating him and electing Franklin D. Roosevelt as president instead. General MacArthur's role in leading the U.S. Army attack on the Bonus Army ended his own chance of ever winning the White House.

The Bonus Army march on Washington focused American attention on the veterans' grievances. Although they did not succeed in winning the promised bonus, they did help get rid of the Hoover administration. Roosevelt's New Deal program then provided federal emergency relief for the jobless and created new government jobs for millions of people.

THE NEWARK SIX-DAY RIOT

Newark, New Jersey, was seething one hot July because of black complaints about police brutality. But the African-Americans there had even deeper grievances. The city had twenty-four thousand unemployed black adults, and twenty thousand jobless black teenagers had no place to go and nothing to do. Despair was the order of the day in the black community.

An angry mob of African-Americans quickly formed after white police were seen clubbing and kicking a black cab driver as they dragged him into a police station. The mob threw firebombs against the station wall. It burst into flame. The rioters then hurled a barrage of rocks. Police charged out, clubbing everyone within reach. That triggered a six-day riot of rock throwing, firebombing, window smashing, looting, and car burning.

Some three hundred state troopers and twenty-six hundred national guardsmen had to reinforce Newark's fourteen-hundred-man police force. The streets echoed with persistent gunfire, most of it aimed at looters. Many wild bullets struck innocent people.

Rumors of African-American snipers made the young, inexperienced guardsmen nervous and trigger-happy. When they mistook one of their own men for a sniper they poured fire into a housing project, killing several men, women, and children.

"You have now created a state of hysteria," Newark's police chief raged at the guardsmen. He later said in disgust, "Guardsmen were firing upon police and police were firing back."

State troopers shot at African-Americans standing on their own porches. Guardsmen fired into a passing car, killing a 10-year-old boy. They shot and killed an 11-year-old boy whose mother had sent him out with the garbage. Guardsmen and troopers rode around in Jeeps, firing into stores with SOUL BROTHER signs in the window. Some seized black youths, put pistols to their heads, forced them to say foul things about their race, then terrified them by pulling the trigger on an empty chamber.

When the Newark riot finally ended, twenty-one African-Americans had been killed, including six women and two children. Over one thousand people had been injured and sixteen hundred were arrested. Over ten million dollars' worth of property had been burned or looted.

The year was 1967. Black despair had grown so great that fully 233 riots erupted that year, involving 168 cities.

DETROIT: "IT LOOKED LIKE THE CITY HAD BEEN BOMBED"

Only a few days after the Newark riot another riot erupted, this time in Detroit. It was sparked by a police raid on a black after-hours drinking club during which seventy-three people were arrested. Rumors of police brutality spread through the neighborhood.

A mob began hurling bricks through shop windows and looting the stores. They threw firebombs, and a high wind swept the flames through the city. When firefighters raced to fight the blazes, rioters drove them off with rocks.

Overwhelmed Detroit police felt helpless to cope with the riot. Michigan Governor George Romney proclaimed a state of emergency and rushed in eight thousand national guardsmen and state troopers. Washington dispatched forty-seven hundred federal paratroopers to Detroit. This force battled the rampaging mobs.

They sprayed bullets wildly at real or imagined snipers, killing many innocent people, as the guard had done in Newark. Some snipers did attack police, firemen, and guardsmen. The guardsmen's Patton tanks rumbled through the streets with machine guns blazing, strafing buildings suspected of harboring snipers.

One young guardsman declared grimly, "I'm gonna shoot anything that moves and is black!"

Many of the African-Americans killed were found to be unarmed. Police arrested over seventy-two hundred and beat many in police stations to force confessions. One guardsman from a small town in northern Michigan declared the action of the Detroit police "brutal and hateful. Police hate Negroes extremely and enjoy the opportunity."

Another guardsman said that the riots had changed his attitude about blacks by "opening my eyes to the conditions Negroes live under."

Of forty-three people killed in the riot, thirty-three were black. Two thousand people were injured. The federal paratroopers finally restored order, following strict instructions not to fire indiscriminately at buildings, cars, or mobs.

The riot had lasted five days. Governor Romney flew over the city to assess the damage. "It looked like the city had been bombed . . . with entire blocks in flames," he said. Insurance for property damage was estimated at thirty-two million dollars. Five thousand people were left homeless.

"WHY IS THERE A VIOLENCE OF DESPAIR?"

In the 1950s and 1960s African-Americans had been promised equal opportunities in jobs, housing, and schools. Some progress had been made. Many blacks had made their way into the middle class. But most found themselves still continuing to live in the same intolerable conditions of grinding poverty.

Commentators agreed that the basic reason for the riots in Newark and Detroit was despair in the black communities.

"Why is there a violence of despair?" asked William Stringfellow sarcastically, in an article in the *Notre Dame Lawyer*. ". . . Why should there be despair for a boy who . . . graduated from high school—and has only the equivalent of a sixth-grade education—and who then cannot find a job, not only because he is Negro, but because there are no jobs for what skills he has? Why should there be a violence of despair? As someone has said, because the people are sick and tired, and they are sick and tired of being sick and tired."

Congress was so angered by the ghetto riots in Newark and Detroit that it voted down President Johnson's extended civil rights program. Thus the rioters not only precipitated violence against their own black community but also lost benefits that Congress had been prepared to extend to them.

"WERE WE BECOMING CONDITIONED TO VIOLENCE?"

Less than one year later infuriated African-American mobs rioted again, in the ghettos of 125 cities in twenty-eight states. The spark that ignited them was the April 1968 assassination, by a white sniper, of the Reverend Martin Luther King, one of the nation's foremost black leaders and a preacher of nonviolence.

"Perhaps the most disturbing thing about the April riots," said President Johnson, "was the fact that so many of us almost instinctively expected them to happen as soon as the news of Dr. King's death was made known. Were we becoming conditioned to violence?"

Black Power advocate Stokely Carmichael fed black shock and rage. "If you don't have a gun, go home." he cried to mobs in the capital's sprawling ghetto. "When the white man comes he is coming to kill you. I don't want any black blood in the street. Go home and get you a gun and then come back, because I got *me* a gun!" He brandished a pistol.

Roving bands of African-American teenagers descended on Washington's downtown shopping district. They lighted vengeful fires that blazed against the night sky. The small capital police force went on alert as arson was followed by break-ins and looting.

The turmoil persisted through the dawn. It increased all the next day as looters dashed in and out of shattered shop windows, carrying off booty in plain sight of the police.

They set seventy new fires. Water pressure ran low as firemen desperately battled the conflagrations to keep Washington from being razed to the ground. The fires and rioting spread dangerously close to the White House.

President Johnson declared the capital endangered by "violence and disorder." He ordered out sixty-six hundred army and National Guard troops. Helmeted combat forces guarded the White House, bayoneted rifles at the ready. Once again a machine-gun post defended the steps of the Capitol.

Troops and police gradually brought the mobs under control, after over thirteen million dollars' worth of damage. The president imposed a dusk-to-dawn curfew on the capital.

He recalled later: "I remember the sick feeling that came over me . . . as I saw the black smoke from burning buildings fill the sky over Washington. And as I watched armed troops patrolling the streets of the nation's capital for the first time since the Civil War, I wondered, as every American must have wondered, what we were coming to."

Similar riots exploded in 124 other cities.

"Police-control problems exceeded anything ever before experienced," noted Attorney General Ramsey Clark. "Traffic stopped, stores closed, windows were smashed, there was looting, arson and finally deadly violence—all to honor the fallen prophet of nonviolence. In recurring waves for several days, as if we had been seized by a nationwide fever, there was more rioting, looting and arson."

This time the nation's police forces had begun to learn how to handle mobs appropriately. They largely avoided the risks of overreacting and provoking new and higher levels of violence, as well as inadequate action that could permit small disturbances to escalate quickly into major riots.

That turbulent summer, mobs of white vigilantes armed with shotguns roamed many cities by night. They announced that their purpose was to protect shops from looters and whites from being attacked on streets after dark.

Most white Americans at the time were upset by the ghetto riots and favored harsh "law and order" crackdowns to suppress peaceful demonstrations as well as violent mobs. They voted overwhelmingly for Richard M. Nixon as president, partly because he promised to take a tough line on suppressing dissent and rioting.

The ghetto riots subsided principally because the majority of African-Americans were the ones who had suffered most from the violence. They ardently wanted ghetto mobs to "cool it." Many were tired of being held responsible for the violent actions of a minority. They felt that rioting had only made things worse for African-Americans by stiffening white opposition to equal opportunity for blacks.

Black political leaders began to gain influence in the big cities that had been abandoned by whites fleeing to the suburbs. There was a growing feeling that maybe, after all, there was more to be gained by working for needed changes within the system than by burning it down.

STUDENT RIOTS

In June 1962 college students organized Students for a Democratic Society (SDS) at Port Huron, Michigan, in rebellion against American society, which they perceived as materialistic. They deplored the pursuit of success, money, and possessions. The young men and women, wearing torn blue jeans, sought to "do their own thing" as individuals instead of conforming to the expectations of the Establishment.

They wrote a "Port Huron Statement," asserting that life in the United States filled them with despair. They accused the system of being rigid and outdated; society's leaders of mouthing hypocritical platitudes; and the job opportunities offered to youths of being over-rated and corrupting.

SDS called for mass resistance to make the American government, economy, and universities more responsive to human needs. They condemned the Cold War against the Soviet Union as a bankrupt foreign policy, and they demanded an end to it. Organizing chapters in many colleges, they demanded a voice in university policy-making to stop education from being an impersonal, assembly-line affair.

When police in Berkeley, California, tried to arrest an unauthorized SDS speaker on the university campus, a mob of three thousand students surrounded the police car and refused to let it leave. Philosophy student Mario Savio sprang onto its roof and began a "free speech" rally that lasted for two days. SDS then led sit-in protests in various university buildings.

Police were summoned to clear the students out. SDS responded by calling a general strike that brought the university to a virtual standstill.

"There is a time," Savio told a student mob, "when the operation of the machine becomes so odious, makes you so sick at heart, that you can't take part . . . and you've got to put your bodies on the levers . . . to make it stop."

The strike ended only when University of California President Clark Kerr offered new and liberal rules to accommodate student protest. This victory led to the formation of SDS chapters on most American university campuses.

Student riots in the 1960s and early 1970s followed five years of broken promises by the government of an early end to the hated Vietnam War. Campus explosions occurred when the Johnson and Nixon administrations dragged the war on and on, sending more and more draftees to their deaths. SDS demonstrated against all wars of intervention, claiming such conflicts were encouraged by the big corporations for their own profit.

In addition to demanding an end to the Vietnam War, SDS crusaded for university reform, equal rights for African-Americans, and for human values to take priority over financial concerns.

Campus rioting over these issues occurred chiefly when university presidents called in police and the National Guard, which used violence against the SDS demonstrators.

In April 1968 SDS students at Columbia University, in New York, became outraged by the university's contract to do war research for the Defense Department. To protest they seized five of Columbia's buildings known to hold files proving the militarization of the university. President Grayson Kirk called in police, who broke into the barricaded buildings. They raced through halls and rooms with nightsticks flailing.

The police seized and battered SDS youths, then kicked them down the stairs. A gauntlet of plainclothesmen clubbed them again, handcuffed them, and hauled them roughly off to jail. The bloody confrontation injured 132 students, 4 faculty members, and 12 police. Over 700 SDS members were arrested.

This violation of students' civil right to protest was similar to the violation embodied in the invasion of troops at Kent State in Ohio, except that in this campus invasion no students were murdered. The violence shocked the majority of students and faculty members. Thousands demonstrated in angry protest. President Kirk felt compelled to shut down the university. He estimated damage caused by the student revolt at three hundred thousand dollars. The uproar compelled Kirk to resign that August.

Columbia's example spread to other campuses, which also erupted in stormy demonstrations. But the election of Richard M. Nixon in November 1968 brought only greater suppression and further crackdowns by university administrations. Many in SDS despaired of winning any of their demands.

THE WEATHERMEN: "DAYS OF RAGE"

In April 1969 SDS split apart in a struggle between moderates, who wanted to continue resistance tactics, and frustrated radicals, who now felt that only revolutionary tactics could achieve SDS goals. About fifteen hundred SDS students pulled away to form a new organization: the Weathermen.

They vowed to go underground to fight the Establishment with violent tactics. They made homemade Molotov cocktails—gasoline bombs—from apple-juice bottles and hurled them at police stations, courthouses, and bank offices.

Early in October 1969 some 400 Weathermen went to Chicago to riot in four "Days of Rage." Wearing crash helmets and carrying long nightsticks, they rampaged through the streets, breaking car windshields and store windows. Police shot and wounded 3 and arrested 290.

The despair that drove the Weathermen to use violence against an unheeding administration proved counterproductive. Their rioting only angered the general public, which condemned them—instead of the stubborn Nixon administration.

Some dissenters remained peaceful, refusing to be discouraged by the violent attacks unleashed against them by the government and university administrations. They refused to take the Weatherman path of responding to violence with violence.

By June 1969 a Harris poll showed students in revolt on two out of three American campuses. In the end, however, the peaceful civil disobedience that most deployed was the tactic that improved civil rights, made changes in the university system, forced Lyndon B. Johnson out of the White House, and elected Richard M. Nixon—who claimed to have a secret plan to end the war, making peace a major issue in the 1968 election campaign.

NINE

Other Causes of Riots

One of the strangest American riots resulted from a medical student's gruesome joke. Brandishing a cadaver's arm, he told a little boy it belonged to the child's mother. The boy, whose mother had just died, rushed home in tears and told his father. Outraged, the man had the mother's grave exhumed.

The body was missing. Furious New Yorkers assumed she had been dug up by medical students, along with other cadavers robbed from graves. "Body snatching," they believed, provided cadavers for students to dissect to learn anatomy.

It was 1788. A mob of over a thousand frenzied New Yorkers burst into the hospital. They smashed equipment and attacked medical students. The sheriff had to bundle doctors and students off to jail to protect them. Another mob then attacked the jail, smashing windows and trying to fight their way in.

The mayor called out the militia. But the mob drove the soldiers off with a hail of paving stones. New York's governor sent more troops, ordering them to fire on the rioters. Two volleys felled many in the mob. Panic now swept the rioters, who turned and fled into the night.

Many doctors and medical students were so frightened by the riot against them that they moved to another city.

TWO THOUSAND LYNCHINGS

Some mobs have taken the form of vigilante groups. They seek to avenge alleged crimes against their community or one of their group, or to persecute a hated minority.

In 1835 riverboats were depositing gamblers, robbers, horse thieves, counterfeiters, and desperadoes in the lower southern states. These undesirables were often too shrewd to fall afoul of the law. In desperation local citizens of Vicksburg, Mississippi, formed vigilante mobs that broke into gambling houses to smash and burn gambling equipment. They unceremoniously shot and hanged gamblers.

Two years later a future president, Abraham Lincoln, deplored the "growing disregard for law which pervades the country—the growing disposition to substitute the wild and furious passions in lieu of the sober judgment of courts, and the worse than savage mobs. . . ."

Vigilante mobs also flourished in the frontier towns of the middle and far West. "Necktie parties" formed to hang cattle rustlers and horse thieves. Montana's notorious "Strangler" mobs hanged no less than sixty-three suspects, leaving them swinging from cottonwoods or cabin doors as warnings. "Not with the best judgment in all cases," admitted Theodore Roosevelt, who bought a ranch in the Badlands of South Dakota.

In the last two decades of the nineteenth century, well over two thousand lynchings occurred in the West and the South. Lynch mobs did not limit their victims to men. Their known victims during the nineteenth century included ninety-two women.

MOBS IN THE WHITE HOUSE

Sometimes riots are caused simply when tightly packed crowds panic and turn into violent mobs. On March 4, 1829, over twenty thousand Americans swarmed into Washington to celebrate the inauguration of Andrew Jackson, the "People's President." Statesman and orator Daniel Webster described them as a "monstrous crowd."

Jackson wanted to demonstrate that his administration would represent the common man. He invited the crowds into the White House to join the inaugural celebration.

Thousands responded joyfully. They stood on costly damask-covered chairs with muddy boots and cheered their hero wildly. Many rushed forward to pump his hand, elbowing the rich and fashionable to one side. People shoved, scrambled, and fought to get near the president. Women fainted. Men got bloody noses. Clothing tore. Expensive cut glass and china went splintering against walls and floors.

"I never saw anything like it before!" exclaimed the dazed Webster. A Washington society woman, Mrs. Margaret Bayard Smith, wrote in outrage, "What a pity, what a pity! . . . The whole house had been inundated by the rabble mob. . . . The President, after having been *literally* pressed to death and almost suffocated and torn to pieces in their eagerness to shake hands with Old Hickory, had retreated through the back way and had escaped to his lodgings. . . . Those who got in could not get out by the door again, but had to scramble out of windows."

Officials finally lured the mob out of the White House with tubs of punch planted on the front lawn.

Such riots are worth studying, along with more serious disturbances, because they shed light on the role of mass hysteria in breakdowns of law and order.

RUMORS AND MOBS

Upsetting rumors often spark riots. Many rumors subsequently are found to have no basis in fact. Sometimes they are greatly exaggerated or are only partly true.

In 1935 a five-and-ten-cent store manager in Harlem caught a black youth stealing a penknife. A policeman was called and took the boy to the basement, where he gave him a stern lecture and let him go through a rear entrance. When the boy did not reappear upstairs, a black shopper shrieked that he was being beaten by police in the basement. A rumor then raced through Harlem that a black boy had been murdered by police in the basement of the five-and-ten.

Huge mobs gathered around angry street speakers who called for "wiping out" whites in a race war. Police sought to arrest the speakers. An excited mob of ten thousand blacks surged through Harlem, smashing into, looting, and gutting two hundred white-owned stores. All night long the streets resounded to the crash of windows, the screaming of sirens, and fusillades of shots.

Many blacks fought hand-to-hand battles with the police, who killed three rioters and wounded thirty others. Over two hundred blacks and whites needed treatment for injuries, and over one hundred blacks were arrested. Property damage was estimated at two million dollars.

"MARTIAN INVADERS"

One of the most unusual mob riots in American history occurred in 1938, as Americans were suffering national jitters brought on by Adolf Hitler's threats of world conquest.

On Sunday, October 30, Orson Welles, young director of the "Mercury Theatre" radio program, broadcast a highly realistic dramatization of H. G. Wells's science fiction thriller *War of the Worlds*. After the initial announcement, the CBS program pretended to offer an hour of dance music. It was constantly interrupted by "news bulletins" about a strange flaming object that had fallen on a New Jersey farm.

Finally a breathless "reporter" described furry-bodied monsters with wet leathery faces and serpentine eyes emerging from a huge cylinder. He also announced the arrival of state police. Then, over terrible screams, he gasped that the monsters had destroyed the police with jets of fire. The monsters were heading his way . . . !

Crashes.

Silence.

When CBS had allegedly "reestablished contact," another hysterical announcer reported that New Jersey was now in the hands of Martians. They had already destroyed seven thousand national guardsmen. More cylinders were landing. The highways were clogged with fleeing civilians. An actor pretending to be the "U.S. secretary of the interior" interrupted to appeal for national calm.

By this time wild panic was sweeping many parts of the United States. Listeners who had tuned in late were convinced that they were hearing real news flashes. Others, incredibly, *forgot* the opening announcement that the broadcast was fictional.

Rumors of the "Martian invasion" spread like wildfire. The greatest hysteria broke out in New Jersey and New York. Frightened callers everywhere jammed police switchboards, seeking information on where it was safest to flee. Others phoned in "eyewitness" reports of battles between Martians and earthlings. Doctors everywhere had their hands full treating people for shock and hysteria.

In Jersey City police had to plead with frantic mobs to get off the streets. In Orange, New Jersey, an excited motorist made a theater audience stampede by rushing in to shout that the Martians were invading the state. In Alabama and Virginia frightened mobs gathered in the streets to pray for deliverance.

In Detroit and other midwestern cities wild mobs ran through the streets looting and rioting while some women and children hid in the churches. Some mobs of farmers carried pitchforks and hunting rifles to fight the invading hordes of creatures from outer space.

By morning radio broadcasts and newspapers managed to calm the nation with assurances that no Martians had invaded the earth. Most people who had panicked felt foolish. Some were furious, like the farmer who had thrown up a fort of sandbags, which he had manned all night, keeping guard with a shotgun and pitchfork.

Mobs excited into rioting by a rumor rarely take the time or trouble to check out the truth.

ROCK CONCERTS AND MOB VIOLENCE

When the British rock group the Who played in Cincinnati in 1979, almost seven thousand fans sought to jam through the two banks of doors. They heard the band practicing and thought the concert had begun. Impatient fans battered a locked door, shattering its glass. A stampede began.

When the riot ended, eleven young people aged fifteen to twenty-two were dead, suffocated in the crush. More than twenty others had been injured. The arena was piled ankle high with purses, coats, shoes, and eyeglasses.

"I didn't even move my feet," said Nancy Tyler, 19, of Covington, Kentucky. "One moment I was maybe two hundred feet from the door and the next thing, I was stacked up like kindling. I don't know, but I'd bet there were six or eight people under me."

As a result of this riot Ohio legislators called for a ban on first-come, first-served "festival" seating, which they considered a contributing factor to the riot. The mayor of Providence, Rhode Island, canceled the Who concert scheduled for that city the following week.

In 1986 the rap group Run–D.M.C. gave a concert in the Long Beach Arena, near Los Angeles. It attracted a mob of three hundred members of black and Latino street gangs. They swarmed through the crowd, attacking everyone around them. Audience members struck back, swinging their metal chairs. One man was stabbed and forty-five people were injured. Public Safety Commissioner John Norton of Pittsburgh declared, "There is absolutely no doubt in my mind that rap music spurs violence."

In 1991 the hard-rock group Guns N' Roses gave a concert in Maryland Heights, Missouri. Lead singer Axl Rose became angered when someone in the audience sought to film him. He jumped off the stage and landed on top of the fan. Bodyguards pulled him off. But then the musicians packed their instruments and stalked offstage, leaving behind twenty thousand outraged fans.

The audience went wild, pelting the stage with bottles, cans, rocks, and garbage. Yanking out hundreds of seats, they trashed or stole speakers, video screens, and sound equipment.

Security guards tried to turn fire hoses on the mob. The rioters seized the hoses and turned them back on the guards. A force of five hundred police officers arrived, wading into the mob with nightsticks.

Over sixty young people needed treatment for injuries. Police made sixteen arrests. Property damage was estimated at over two hundred thousand dollars.

There seem to be several reasons for riots at rock and rap concerts. Los Angeles Police Captain Keith Bushey pointed out, "You can't put that many people in that small an area for that period of time without something giving way."

SPORTS EVENTS AND MOB VIOLENCE

Sports fans also become rioting mobs on occasion, especially after championship games. Sometimes ardent fans are chagrined when their team loses, so they attack opposing fans or stadium attendants who try to restrain them. Sometimes they pour out on the field to attack umpires or referees who have made crucial decisions with which they vehemently disagree. And often they stage frenzied violent demonstrations to celebrate their team's victory.

Fan violence is not particularly new. In the nineteenth century authorities in the United States banned boxing because of fan violence that followed the fights.

More recently, in February 1993, a crowd of four hundred thousand fans celebrated the Dallas Cowboys' Super Bowl victory. Fans attacked bystanders, injuring twenty-six. Police arrested twenty-five people.

In 1992 when the Chicago Bulls won their second straight National Basketball Association championship, their rioting fans injured 107 officers who were trying to control the mob.

The violence was even worse when the Bulls won the championship again in 1993 for the third straight year. Fans pulled drivers from their cars, shot one man to death, and stabbed another. The stabbed victim, Oswaldo Arroyo, 17, declared, "They used the victory as an excuse to go out and do what they want." Three women were shot, one fatally.

"It's just senseless," Police Sergeant Wilson McGee said.

Three police officers suffered gunshot wounds, and three others were hit by rocks and bottles. Police in riot gear, on horseback and with police dogs, arrested 682 people, 164 of whom were charged with felonies.

The city had to pay a million dollars in overtime pay for the police. Many storeowners boarded up windows and hired private security guards to protect their stores overnight.

"Let's not forget," declared Associated Press reporter Fred Bayles, "the word 'fan,' as in sports fan, is a shortened form of 'fanatic.'"

Riotous behavior by sports fans is partly the result of fanatical team loyalty and partly the result of the adrenaline rush that comes with taking part in violence.

"Arousal leads to a loss of one's sense of control," explains Delia S. Saenz, a University of Notre Dame social psychologist, about sports fans. "People do what they wouldn't normally do because the person is no longer an individual, no one person is *responsible* for what everyone is doing."

Richard Lapchick, director of Northeastern University's Center for the Study of Sports in Society, sees a mob's victory celebration as a way of allowing fans to work off the frustrations of everyday life. Being part of a crowd gives some a license to misbehave.

"It's a situation where people act in ways they wouldn't on a day-to-day basis," Lapchick explains. "They think that they can do on this particular night something they can't do on another night."

These fans have such a strong identity with their favorite team that they often feel the team's championship victory makes *them* powerful and gives *them* the right to do whatever they want, however violent.

MOB VIOLENCE AND THE MOVIES

Violence has also erupted at movie houses showing films dealing with gang violence. In March 1991 it broke out in over ten cities where the film *New Jack City* was playing. In Brooklyn teenage gangs from rival housing projects fired more than one hundred shots during the screening of the movie, killing one man and wounding a pregnant woman. The manager of the Duffield Twin Theater likened the riot to "World War III."

A few months later, when a film called *Boyz N the Hood* opened, gunfire and pandemonium broke out around the nation at movie theaters showing it.

Warrington Hudlin, president of the Black Filmmaker Foundation, observed, "Each time these movies open up, by this new generation of black filmmakers, there's a huge, huge demand. People are standing in line for hours, and then they're told the theater's out of tickets. You can't frustrate people that way, particularly a segment of the population that has anger anyway."

When an individual is severely frustrated by some occurrence, he is usually unlikely to start a riot by himself. But if people become frustrated as a crowd, they can seek protection in their numbers, and violence often quickly results.

ELECTION RIOTS

Violent mobs have often played an important role in elections. Colonial political parties used mobs to terrorize opponents away from the polls. One of the first election riots occurred in 1742 in the Pennsylvania colony, when Scotch-Irish frontiersmen who made up the Proprietary party sought to oust the Quakers for refusing to fight Indians in the West.

The Proprietary party organized a mob of seventy sailors, arming them with clubs that, one account recorded, they "flourished over their heads with loud huzzas, and in a furious and tumultuous manner approached the place of election." The polls were on a balcony of the courthouse, to which voters mounted from a street staircase. The mob seized and blocked the staircase, clubbing and driving off all Quakers seeking to vote.

But the ordinarily nonviolent Quakers quickly organized a mob of vigilantes of their own. Their mob threw the sailors off the staircase and locked up fifty of them. The election then proceeded peacefully, with a Quaker victory.

Mob murders on election day were commonplace during the 1840s and 1850s. Democrats had succeeded in organizing the immigrant vote in big cities. The Know-Nothing party intensified its efforts to keep foreign-born voters from the polls.

The worst election riots took place in St. Louis, Missouri, in August 1854. Know-Nothings there spread rumors that the Irish were stacking arms in St. Patrick's church and that an Irishman had stabbed a Know-Nothing in the back. Neither rumor was true, but a mob armed with axes attacked rows of Irish houses, demolishing sixty. A quickly formed Irish mob fought back.

"For forty-eight hours," reported a St. Louis newspaper, "the city has been the scene of one of the most appalling riots that has ever taken place in the country. Men have been butchered like cattle, property destroyed, and anarchy reigns supreme. . . . The military and police here have, thus far, been unable to check the onward march of lawlessness and crime. The scenes of last night were terrible, never, we hope, to be enacted again."

Ten people died, and thirty were seriously wounded.

Fortunately for the country, the election-day riots of yesterday are now only memories from a turbulent past.

T E N

What Does Mob Violence Accomplish?

When riots occur, the media bear a special responsibility. If the press, TV, and radio continually report on minorities in a biased way, they may reinforce prejudices and eventually provoke mob violence. Media coverage of a riot may also be inflammatory. The media may intensify or prolong a riot if they spread rumors or exaggerate disturbances for the sake of a sensational news story. This is what happened in newspaper coverage of the labor riots in the 1930s.

Matters are not helped when TV viewers witness supermarkets burning, bricks shattering plate-glass windows, and streets turning into blazing battlegrounds. The public often reacts to such situations with horror and demands stricter law enforcement. That in turn can lead to repression, violations of civil liberties, and eventually even greater riots of protest. Media coverage may inadvertently contribute to the spread of street violence.

In both the 1965 and the 1992 Watts riots, rioters were able to watch their own actions on TV. Continuous TV and radio coverage also revealed police movements. This enabled rioters to judge when and where it was safe to attack, loot, and burn stores.

Nevertheless, the media have a responsibility to keep the public fully and honestly informed. Whether they can do that without adding to the problem or participating in it remains to be seen.

SCAPEGOATS

Once a mob flames into action, their riot feeds on the larger fuel beneath the tinder—unresolved grievances. Deep-rooted cultural animosity is a factor in many riots. A black mob's rage may be fueled by centuries of remembered oppression and discrimination. The violence against the Catholic convent was the result of deep-seated prejudice by Boston Protestants.

As *Newsweek* observed in 1992, "Over the past century there have been four cycles of major riots involving race . . . and each time things seem to cut to the same pattern: a long accumulation of grievances at the bottom, a studied indifference at the top, finally a catalyst— then an explosion. How awful, everyone says. Then the rush to find scapegoats instead of solutions begins."

Most people who participate in mob violence belong to an "in-between" class. They are between the privileged group that oppresses them and an emerging group below that threatens their security. The emerging group frequently contains new immigrants of different ethnicity or race who then compete for jobs and social services. Often the in-between group doesn't dare challenge the ruling class on whom they depend for jobs. So they take out their frustrations and anxieties on the scapegoat class below them.

Thus, when many Protestant workers in the cities felt exploited by nineteenth-century industrialists, they rioted against the newly arrived Catholics whom they saw to be threatening their jobs. Similarly, in the Draft Riots of 1863, New York's Irish Catholics, exploited by a Protestant aristocracy, vented their wrath on black workers brought in as strikebreakers.

In recent years African-Americans who have long suffered discrimination have turned violent against Korean immigrants who have successfully started retail businesses in predominantly black neighborhoods. According to the National Korean American Grocers Association, between 1980 and 1990 forty Korean merchants were shot or injured during robbery attempts by African-Americans.

In 1991 Korean grocer Soon Ja Du incorrectly suspected a 15-year-old black girl, Latasha Harlins, of stealing a bottle of orange juice, and she shot and killed her. African-Americans threatened to boycott and bomb her store, forcing her to shut down. Soon Ja Du was convicted of manslaughter.

The irony of hostility between African-Americans and Koreans is that both have suffered discrimination because of race. Koreans claim that when they first arrived in the United States, they—like many southern blacks—had been refused service in restaurants, theaters, and other public facilities.

At different times victims and aggressors are interchangeable, minority victims becoming aggressors against other minorities.

Another case in point is the hostility of some African-Americans toward Jews. On August 19, 1991, one car in a Hasidic Jewish funeral procession accidentally ran over and killed a 7-year-old African-American boy, Gavin Cato, and seriously injured his 7-year-old cousin Angela. A rumor spread through the largely black Crown Heights neighborhood of New York that a Hasidic-run ambulance had tended to the Hasidic car driver and ignored the black children. African-Americans rioted through the neighborhood for three nights, torching cars and buildings. A Hasidic scholar, Yankel Rosenbaum, was stabbed to death. Before 1,500 riot-clad police took back the streets, 163 people were arrested, and 66 civilians and 173 police were injured.

Hasidic Jews complained that they were constantly victimized by African-Americans, who in turn charged that the Hasidim received preferential treatment by the city.

WHEN PROMISES TO GROUPS ARE BROKEN

Angry mobs grow out of dissatisfied groups of people when official promises of reform are not followed by action.

"Most groups which have engaged in mass violence," observed Richard E. Rubenstein, consultant to the Kerner Commission, "have done so only after a long period of fruitless, relatively nonviolent struggle in which established procedures have been tried and found wanting."

When groups become strong and united enough, they may lash back at oppressors with riots of their own. Participation in such mobs is a means of expressing hostility, rebellion, and desire for revenge. It also establishes pride of identity in a race, religion, occupation, or cause that may be scorned by the majority. Rioting gives underdogs a new sense of power. They become aware that they can strike fear into the hearts of their opponents.

But history shows us that after the riot—with a few notable exceptions—little or nothing happens to improve the situation. And often the community that suffers the most after the riot is the rioters' own.

In general, nonviolent demonstrations are much more likely to produce change. The peaceful demonstrations led by Martin Luther King, Jr., gradually turned public opinion against racism and restrictive laws. They helped lay the groundwork for civil rights legislation that enabled millions of African-Americans to rise out of poverty into the middle class.

Some authorities believe that no concessions should ever be made to mobs that riot, no matter how valid their grievances. To do so, they warn, would legitimize or reward violence and undermine respect for law and order.

"I have always been taught," declared former Supreme Court Justice Tom Clark in 1970, "that this nation was dedicated to freedom *under law*, not under mobs."

His son, former Attorney General Ramsey Clark, held a somewhat different view. "From one side of America's house," he said, "we hear the demand for order: There must be order! It is the voice of those who resist change. From the other side of our house comes the plea for justice: Give us justice! This is the voice of those who seek change. But the long history of mankind says you will have neither order nor justice unless you have both."

Senator Bill Bradley of New Jersey observed in 1992 that to avoid future riots we need to spend much more than we do now on the Job Corps, neighborhood development, unemployment benefits, welfare reform, and care for the children of working mothers.

We also need to do more to prevent the violence that results from racism and intolerance by educating each new generation in our homes and schoolrooms in the traditions of fair play. We need to understand that everyone in our country—regardless of race, religion, or life-style—is entitled to the respect that we expect ourselves. Getting to know people of other races, religions, and life-styles in our everyday lives is the best way of seeing them as individuals rather than stereotypes.

Repressive taxes still plague Americans, but fortunately most modern protests are nonviolent. Unpopular court decisions, however, still provoke violent demonstrations, as in the case of Operation Rescue, which opposes the Supreme Court's decision legalizing abortion. The best way to prevent such demonstrations is to oppose the use of violence, as many other antiabortion groups did publicly. Pro-choice advocates in the dispute over abortion are pledged to nonviolent demonstrations.

Instead of taking to the streets, those who complain of social injustice need to make powerful but nonviolent appeals in the court of public opinion. Reason will eventually win where rage and riots have most often failed.

BIBLIOGRAPHY AND
RECOMMENDED READING

Introduction

*Block, Irvin. *Violence in America.* New York: Public Affairs Committee, 1970.

*Chaplin, J. P. *Rumor, Fear and the Madness of Crowds.* New York: Ballantine Books, 1959.

*Fogelson, Robert M. *Violence as Protest.* Greenwood, Ill.: Greenwood Press, 1971.

*Higham, Robin, ed. *Bayonets in the Streets.* Manhattan, Kansas: Sunflower University Press, 1989.

*Miller, David L. *Introduction to Collective Behavior.* Prospect Heights, Ill.: Waveland Press, 1989.

Rosenthal, Uriel, et al., eds. *Coping with Crises: The Management of Disasters, Riots and Terrorism.* Springfield, Ill.: Charles C. Thomas, 1989.

Rule, James B. *Theories of Civil Violence.* Berkeley: University of California Press, 1988.

Yablonsky, Lewis. *The Violent Gang.* Baltimore, Md.: Penguin Books, 1966.

1. When Court Decisions Trigger Violence

*Archer, Jules. *1968: Year of Crisis.* New York: Julian Messner, 1971.

*———. *Resistance.* Philadelphia: Macrae Smith Company, 1973.

*National Commission on the Causes and Prevention of Violence. *Rights in Conflict (Walker Report).* New York: New American Library, 1968.

* indicates recommended reading

*Sherrill, Robert. *Gothic Politics in the Deep South*. New York: Vintage Books, 1968.
Silberman, Charles E. *Crisis in Black and White*. New York: Vintage Books, 1964.

2. When Intolerance Leads to Violence

*Archer, Jules. *The Chinese and the Americans*. New York: Hawthorn Books, 1976.
*———. *The Extremists*. New York: Hawthorn Books, 1969.
*———. *Riot!* New York: Hawthorn Books, 1974.
*Bisson, Wilfred J. *Countdown to Violence: The Charlestown Convent Riot of 1834*. New York: Garland Publishers, 1989.
Markmann, Charles Lam. *The Noblest Cry*. New York: St. Martin's Press, 1965.
*Myers, Gustavus. *History of Bigotry in the United States*. New York: Capricorn Books, 1960.
*Sinkler, George. *The Racial Attitudes of American Presidents*. Garden City, N.Y.: Doubleday, 1971.

3. When Racial Prejudice Creates Violence

*Archer, Jules. *Angry Abolitionist: William Lloyd Garrison*. New York: Julian Messner, 1969.
———. *Mexico and the United States*. New York: Hawthorn Books, 1973.
Blassingame, John W. *The Slave Community: Plantation Life in the Antebellum South*. New York: Oxford University Press, 1972.
*Grimshaw, Allen D. *Racial Violence in the United States*. Chicago: Aldine Publishing, 1969.
Gunther, John. *Inside U.S.A.* New York: Bantam Books, 1942.
*Headley, Joel Tyler. *The Great Riots of New York: 1712 to 1873*. New York: New American Library, 1965.
*Mazon, Mauricio. *The Zoot-Suit Riots: The Psychology of Symbolic Annihilation*. Austin: University of Texas Press, 1984.
*Schwartz, Barry N., and Robert Disch. *White Racism: Its History, Pathology and Practice*. New York: Dell Publishing, 1970.
Segal, Ronald. *The Race War*. New York: Viking Press, 1967.
*Waskow, Arthur. *From Race Riot to Sit-In*. Hapeville, Ga.: P. Smith, 1975.

4. When Americans Fear Losing Their Jobs

Allen, Frederick Lewis. *Only Yesterday*. New York: Bantam Books, 1946.
Chute, William J. *The American Scene: 1860 to the Present*. New York: Bantam Books, 1966.
Hofstadter, Richard, ed. *Great Issues in American History: A Documentary Record*. New York: Vintage Books, 1969.

*Lens, Sidney. *Poverty Yesterday and Today*. New York: Thomas Y. Crowell, 1973.

Leuchtenburg, William E. *Franklin D. Roosevelt and the New Deal*. New York: Harper & Row, 1963.

*Shannon, David A. *The Great Depression*. Englewood Cliffs, N.J.: Prentice-Hall, 1960.

5. *When Police Turn Violent*

*Archer, Jules. *The Incredible Sixties: The Stormy Years that Changed America*. San Diego: Harcourt Brace Jovanovich, 1986.

*———. *Strikes, Bombs and Bullets*. New York: Julian Messner, 1972.

*Black, Algernon D. *The People and the Police*. New York: McGraw-Hill, 1968.

Commager, Henry Steele. *Freedom and Order*. Cleveland: World Publishing, 1968.

*Epstein, Jason. *The Great Conspiracy Trial*. New York: Random House, 1970.

*Graham, Hugh Davis, and Ted Robert Gurr. *The History of Violence in America*. New York: Bantam Books, 1969.

Report of the National Advisory Commission on Civil Disorders (Kerner Report). New York: Pantheon, 1988.

*Stein, David Lewis. *Living the Revolution: The Yippies in Chicago*. Indianapolis: Bobbs-Merrill, 1969.

6. *When Taxes Become Oppressive*

*Archer, Jules. *They Made a Revolution: 1776*. New York: Scholastic, 1973.

*———. *The Unpopular Ones*. New York: Crowell-Collier, 1968.

Chute, William J. *The American Scene: 1600–1860*. New York: Bantam Books, 1966.

Dorson, Richard M., ed. *America Rebels*. New York: Pantheon, 1953.

Scheer, George F., and Hugh F. Rankin. *Rebels and Redcoats*. New York: New American Library, 1959.

7. *When Americans Clash over War*

Archer, Jules. *Fighting Journalist: Horace Greeley*. New York: Julian Messner, 1966.

*———. *Hawks, Doves and the Eagle*. New York: Hawthorn Books, 1970.

———. *Treason in America*. New York: Hawthorn Books, 1971.

*———. *World Citizen: Woodrow Wilson*. New York: Julian Messner, 1967.

*Becker, Howard S., ed. *Campus Power Struggle*. Chicago: Aldine, 1970.

*Lukas, J. Anthony. *Don't Shoot—We Are Your Children!* New York: Dell, 1972.

Osborne, John. *The Second Year of the Nixon Watch*. New York: Liveright, 1971.

Pullen, John J. *Patriotism in America*. New York: American Heritage Press, 1971.

Spender, Stephen. *The Year of the Young Rebels*. New York: Vintage Books, 1969.

*Stone, I. F. *The Killings at Kent State*. New York: New York Review, 1971.

*Wills, Garry. *The Second Civil War*. New York: New American Library, 1968.

8. When Despair Breeds Violence

*Archer, Jules. *The Plot to Seize the White House.* New York: Hawthorn Books, 1971.
*————. *Revolution in Our Time.* New York: Julian Messner, 1971.
 Blaustein, Albert P., and Robert L. Zangrando, eds. *Civil Rights and the Black American.* New York: Simon and Schuster, 1970.
 Conant, Ralph W. *The Prospects for Revolution.* New York: Harper's Magazine Press, 1971.
*Grant, Joanne, ed. *Black Protest.* New York: Fawcett Premier, 1968.
 Lasch, Christopher. *The New Radicalism in America.* New York: Vintage Books, 1967.
 Miles, Michael W. *The Radical Probe.* New York: Atheneum, 1971.
 Polenberg, Richard. *One Nation Divisible.* New York: Penguin Books, 1980.

9. Other Causes of Riots

*Archer, Jules. *Winners and Losers.* San Diego: Harcourt Brace Jovanovich, 1984.
*Heaps, Willard Allison. *Riots, U.S.A., 1765–1970.* New York: Seabury Press, 1970.
*Heffner, Richard D., and Michael Wallace, eds. *American Violence.* New York: Vintage Books, 1971.
*Jain, Uday. *The Psychological Consequences of Crowding.* Newbury Park, Ca.: Sage Publications, 1988.
*Le Bon, Gustave. *The Crowd.* Marietta, Ga.: Cherokee Publishing, 1982.
*Loo, Chalsa M., ed. *Crowding and Behavior.* New York: Irvington Publishers, 1974.
 Sanders, Helen Fitzgerald, and William H. Bertsche, Jr., eds. *X. Beidler, Vigilante.* Norman: University of Oklahoma Press, 1957.
*Upton, James N. *A Social History of Twentieth-Century Urban Riots.* Bristol, In.: Wyndham Hall Press, 1984.
*Valentine, Alan. *Vigilante Justice.* New York: Reynal & Co., 1956.

10. What Does Mob Violence Accomplish?

*Allen, Bud, and Diana Bosta. *Recognizing Signs of a Riot and What to Do About Them.* New York: Rae John, 1989.
 Brown, Hedy. *People, Groups, and Society.* Philadelphia: Open University Press, 1985.
 Canetti, Elias. *Crowds and Power.* New York: Farrar, Straus and Giroux, 1984.
*Carlsson, Gosta. *Mass Response and Individual Choice.* Philadelphia: Coronet Books, 1987.
 Currey, Cecil B. *Road to Revolution.* New York: Harper & Row, 1971.
*De Bruyn, Lucy. *Mob-Rule and Riots.* New York: New York State Mutual Books, 1984.

Graumann, C. F., and S. Moscovici, eds. *Changing Conceptions of Crowd Mind and Behavior.* New York: Springer-Verlag, 1986.

Leinwand, Gerald, ed. *Civil Rights and Civil Liberties.* New York: Washington Square Press, 1968.

*Rubenstein, Richard E. *Rebels in Eden: Mass Political Violence in the United States.* Boston: Little, Brown, 1970.

Also consulted for all chapters were issues of *The American Legion Magazine; The Center Magazine; Civil Liberties; The Harvard Bulletin; In These Times; The Los Angeles Daily News; The Nation; The New Yorker; New York Magazine; The New York Review of Books; The New York Times; The New York Times Magazine; Newsweek; People; Psychology Today; Rolling Stone; The Santa Cruz [California] Sentinel; The Saturday Evening Post; Sports Illustrated; Time; University: A Princeton Quarterly; USA Weekend;* and *U.S. News and World Report.*

I N D E X

Abolition, 45–48, 104, 118. *See also* Slavery
Abortion, 23–24, 157
Adams, John, 92, 95
Adams, Samuel, 92, 93–94, 95, 96
African-Americans: "Black Codes," 119; education, 118, 132–33; employment, 21, 53–55, 62, 130, 132–33; ghettos, 21–22, 130, 135; and Koreans, 154–55; and Jews, 155; middle class, 58, 132, 156; migration north, 50, 51, 52, 54; mob violence against, 14–15, 41, 48–49, 50–51, 52, 57, 58, 59–61, 105, 106–7, 109, 118, 130, 134–35, 154, 155; mob violence by, 18–20, 41–42, 48–49, 52, 62, 117–18, 133–34, 146–47, 149, 154; and organized labor, 50, 53, 54, 105, 119, 154; political leaders, 20, 133, 135, 156; poverty, 21, 58, 130, 132; Reconstruction, 118–20; segregation, 13–14, 15, 16, 53, 59–60, 155; unequal justice, 23, 51–52, 53, 56, 59–60, 61–62, 118; veterans, 53, 56–57. *See also* Abolition; Slavery
Alabama: and Freedom Riders, 59–60; response to *War of the Worlds,* 145; slavery legislation, 118
American Protective League (APL), 39
American Revolution, 2, 4, 10, 93, 96
Anacostia Flats, 122; troop riot at, 124, 125, 127–28
Antilabor riots, 39–41, 79–81
Antiwar protests, 115. *See also* Civil War; Vietnam War; War of 1812; World War I
Arroyo, Oswaldo, 148
Arthur, Chester, 35
Attucks, Crispus, 92

Bayles, Fred, 148
Bigelow, Herbert, 109
Bilbo, Theodore, 99

Black, Algernon D., 58

Blacks. *See* African-Americans; Slavery

"Body-snatching" riot (New York, 1788), 141–42

Bonus Army, 120–29; and Congress, 120–21, 122, 123; East St. Louis riot, 121; electoral response to, 129; and Herbert Hoover, 122, 123–24, 125; march on Washington, 120-21; rout of, 125–29

Bonus bill, 120–21, 122, 123

Boston riots: antiabolitionist riot, 45–48; Boston Massacre, 91–93, 111; Boston Tea Party, 95–96; Civil War draft riot, 109; colonial agitation against British, 93; Palmer raids, 41; Stamp Act riots, 94–95; Ursuline Convent riot, 27–30

Bradley, Bill, 5, 157

Bradley, Charles C., 101

Brennan, Peter, 114

Britain: colonial agitation against, 93; legislation, 94–95, 96; War of 1812, 104

Brown v. Board of Education, 13

Brown, Richard Maxwell, 3

Burleigh, C. C., 45–46

Bush, George, 19

Bushey, Keith, 147

California: opposition to Chinese immigration, 34; riot against fruit workers, 73. *See also* Los Angeles; San Francisco

Carmichael, Stokely, 133

Carpetbaggers, 119

Catholics: immigration of, 30; prejudice against, 27, 30, 31, 50; violence against, 27–30, 31, 38, 41, 154; violence by, 154

Cato, Gavin, 155

Centralia, Washington: attack on IWW, 40

Charlestown, Massachusetts: *See* Boston riots; Ursuline Convent riot

Chicago, Illinois: Bulls riots (1992, 1993), 148; Cicero riot (1951), 57–58; Days of Rage (1969), 138; Democratic National Convention police riot (1968), 84–88, 113; and the Great Depression, 70, 71; Pullman strike (1894), 67–69, (1919), 52–53; Republic Steel strike, 74–76

Childs, Ted, 62

Chinese-Americans: legislation against, 34–35; prejudice against, 33, 34, 36; strikebreaking, 35, 50; violence against, 32–34, 35–36, 38

Cincinnati, Ohio: race riot (1829), 49; The Who concert riot (1979), 146

CIO (Congress of Industrial Organizations), 74

Civil rights: legislation, 15, 57, 60, 133; violations of, 22, 58, 112, 137. *See also* Dissent; First Amendment rights

Civil War: South and, 50, 119–20; Union draft, 105, 108, 109, 114

Clark, Harvey, 57–58

Clark, Ramsey, 4, 87, 134, 157

Clark, Tom, 156

Class conflict, 5–6, 22, 41–42, 105, 154

Cleveland, Grover, 35, 36, 69

Colonial America. *See* American Revolution; Boston riots; Britain; British troops

Colorado miners' strikes, 82–84

Committees of Correspondence, 93

Committee on Public Information, 39

Communism: fear of, 39–41, 124. *See also* Red-baiting

Connor, "Bull," 59

Constitution, 13, 41. *See also* First Amendment rights

Constitutional Convention, 13

Continental Congress, 10

Conyers, John, 88

Coughlin, Father Charles, 55

Courts: attacks on courthouses, 9, 10, 18, 31, 37, 97, 100, 101; decisions causing violence: 2, 10, 13, 14, 15, 16, 18, 20, 23, 57, 59, 61–62, 157; responses to violence, 12, 15, 17–18, 22–23, 31, 51–52, 58, 61–62, 69, 73, 84, 88, 92–93, 98, 110, 112, 113, 118, 156

Creel, George, 39–40

Crowd control, 3, 134

Crowding and riots, 143, 147, 149

Custom House riot, 91–92; casualties of, 92; judicial response to, 92–93

Daley, Richard, 84–85, 87, 88

Darley, John, 4

Days of Rage, 138

Dearborn, Michigan: Ford massacre, 71–72

Debs, Eugene, 67, 68, 69–70, 110

Democratic National Convention (Chicago, 1968), 84, 85, 87, 113; casualties of riot, 86, 87; Chicago police riot, 85–87, 113; consequences of, 87–88; as "Daley's gift to Nixon," 88; Hubert Humphrey nomination, 84; and media, 86, 87

Democrats, 15, 87, 88, 119

Denny, Reginald Oliver, 19

Deportation of Chinese, 35–36; and World War I, 41, 109

Depression, Great, 71, 77, 99, 121. *See also* Economic riots; Great Depression; New Deal

Deshong, Beatrice, 51

Detroit, Michigan: ghetto riot (1967), 131–32; and Palmer raids, 41; race riot (1943), 54–56; and *War of the Worlds,* 145–46

Dinkins, David, 62

Dissent, 2–3, 11; government suppression of, 39–40, 79, 87–88, 110, 112, 114, 115, 118, 135, 137, 153. *See also* Antiwar protests; First Amendment rights; Police riots

Draft: protest against, 3, 104, 110. *See also* Draft riots

Draft riots: Civil War, 109, 114; New York (1863), 104–9, 154

Duryee, Abram, 80, 81

East St. Louis, Missouri: clash with Bonus Army (1932), 121; race riot (1917), 50–51

Eckford, Elizabeth, 14

Economic hardship: as cause for rioting, 5–6, 10, 58, 65–66, 67–68, 76, 96, 99

Economic reform, 12, 73, 77, 100, 129, 157

Economic riots: Great Depression, 70–73, 99–101, 120–129; New York (1837), 65–66; New York (1874), 79–81; Pullman strike (1894), 67–69. *See also* Unions

Eighth Amendment, 13

Eisenhower, Dwight D., 15, 125

Election-day riots, 31–32, 120, 150–51. *See also* Voting rights

Elections and social change, 70, 135; Great Depression, 100–101, 129; Reconstruction, 120; Shays's Rebellion, 12; Vietnam War protests, 88, 110, 135, 138; Whiskey Rebellion, 98

Ethnic prejudice, 3, 22, 34, 41, 56, 154–55, 157. *See also* Chinese–Americans; Immigrants; Jews; Palmer raids
Evans, Bergen, 1
Everest, Wesley, 40

Fama, Joseph, 61
Farm Holiday riots, 99–101
Farmers: Farm Holiday strikes, 99–101; foreclosures, 9, 10, 99, 100; legislative reforms, 12, 98, 100–101; Shays's Rebellion, 9, 10, 12, 13; and taxes, 10, 96–97, 98, 99; and *War of the Worlds,* 45–46; Whiskey Rebellion, 96–99
Faubus, Orval, 13–15
FBI (Federal Bureau of Investigation), 40, 113
Federal troops: Chicago (1894), 69, (1968), 84; Colorado (1913–1914), 83–84; Detroit (1943), 55, (1967), 131; and GMA, 68; Little Rock (1957), 14–15; Los Angeles (1992), 20; New York City (1863), 106, 107, 108; in South during Reconstruction, 50, 119, 120; Washington, D.C. (1932), 125–29, (1968), 134; and Whiskey Rebellion, 98
Federal troop riots, 69, 125–29
Federalist party, 98
First Amendment rights, 1, 87, 112, 137
Flint, Michigan: GM strike, 74
Flour riot, 65–66
Ford plant: riot at, 71–72
Frank, Leo, 37–38
Frankfurter, Felix, 41
Freedom Riders, 59–60
Frustration: and violence, 149–150, 156

Gangs, 18–19, 146, 149
Garfield, James A., 34
Garrison, William Lloyd, 45–48, 118
Gates, Daryl, 17, 19, 20
General Managers' Association (GMA), 68–69
General Motors strike, 74
Georgia: lynching in, 38, 57
German-Americans: attacks on, 39–40
Ghetto riots, 4, 21, 58, 132–33; Detroit (1967), 131–32; King assassination (1968), 133–135; Newark (1967), 130–31; Watts (1965), 21, (1992), 18–20, 21–22
Gil, Robert, 19
Girdler, Tom, 74
Glassford, Pelham, 122
Goddard, Louisa, 28
Gompers, Samuel, 80, 81
Grant, Ulysses S., 80
Greeley, Horace, 105
Griffith, Michael, 61
Gunn, David, 24
Gunther, John, 56

Hamilton, Alexander, 97–98
Hancock, John, 95
Hardhat riot, 113–14
Harding, Warren, 70
Harlem, New York, riot (1935), 144
Harlins, Latasha, 155
Hart & Company, 65–66
Hawkins, Yusuf, 60–62
Hayes, Rutherford B., 34–35, 39
Hitler, Adolf, 55, 144
Holliday, George, 17; video made by, 17, 22
Homelessness, 81–82. *See also* Housing
Hoover, Herbert, 121–25, 129
Hoover, J. Edgar, 40

Housing, 132; competition for, 41, 52, 58, cost of, 21–22; loss of, 66, 70–71, 81–82
Hudlin, Warrington, 149
Humphrey, Hubert, 84
Hurley, Pat, 128–29
Hutchinson, Thomas, 92, 94, 95

Immigrants, 41, 58; and African-Americans, 22, 52, 154–55; Chinese, 32–36; German, 39; Irish, 30–31, 150; Jews, 37; Korean, 154–55; and labor, 30, 31, 33, 34; and Palmer raids, 39, 40, 41; and vigilantes, 39. *See also* by ethnic group; "Know-Nothings"; Workingmen's Party
Integration: as leading to racial tolerance, 62, 157; of neighborhoods, 57–58, 62; of schools, 13, 16; of swimming pools, 57; of workplace, 62
Irish-Americans, 30–31, 41, 105, 150
IWW (Industrial Workers of the World): attacks on, 39, 40

Jackson inauguration riot, 143
Jackson, Andrew "Old Hickory," 143
Jackson, Reverend Jesse, 20
Javits, Jacob, 114
Jefferson, Thomas, 11, 98
Jews: anti-Semitism, 37, 38, 50, 55, 155; immigration of, 37; violence against, 37–38, 41, 155
Jim Crow laws, 53, 55
Johnson, Lyndon B.: civil rights program, 133; Democratic National Convention (1968), 87; single term, 110, 138; and studies on violence, 2, 84
Johnson, Nicholas, 114

Kennedy, John A., 105
Kennedy, Robert, 59
Kent State University, killings, 111–113, 114, 115, 137
Kerner Commission, 2, 53, 156
Kim, Charles, 19
King, Martin Luther, Jr.: assassination of, 133; and nonviolence, 134, 156
King, Rodney, 17–18, 20, 22–23; verdict riot, 18–20, 76
"Know-Nothings," 31; and election-day riots, 150–51
Knox, Henry, 11
Korean-Americans, 19, 22, 154–155
Kotkin, Joel, 22
Ku Klux Klan, 50

Labor riots, 34, 76–77; Rock Springs (1885), 35; East St. Louis (1917), 50–51. *See also* Antilabor riots; Strikes; Unions
La Follette, Robert, 75–76
Lapchick, Richard, 149
Latané, Bibb, 4
Latinos, 18–19, 22, 54, 146
"Law and order" crackdowns, 4, 88, 135, 153
Law enforcement, 2, 5. *See also* Federal troops; National Guard; Police
Lee, Henry, 98, 104
Legislation: against minorities, 34, 35, 36, 118, 119; inciting riots, 2, 57; responding to riots, 12, 13, 15, 22, 73, 77, 94, 96, 100, 101, 109, 114, 118, 121–123, 133, 146, 156
Levy, Sheldon G., 2
Light, Ivan, 22
Lincoln, Abraham, 105, 108, 142
Linderfelt, K. E., 83, 84
Lindsay, John, 113–114

Little Rock, Arkansas, 13; Central
High riots, 13–16
Looting, 3, 22; of food, 66, 69, 70, 72;
and media coverage of riots, 153;
occurrences of, 19, 29, 56, 58, 97,
107, 108, 117, 130, 131, 133, 134, 144,
146
Los Angeles, California: anti-Chinese
riots (1871), 32; King verdict riot
(1992), 18–20, 22, 153; settlements
for police brutality, 88; urban
decay, 21–22, 58; Watts riot (1965),
21–22, 153; zoot-suit riots (1943),
54. *See also* Rodney King; Los
Angeles Police Department
Los Angeles Police Department
(LAPD): brutality of, 17, 20, 21; and
"excessive force" lawsuits, 88;
Gates's resignation, 20; and King
verdict riot, 19, 20, 22; training, 20,
22; trials of officers in King beating,
17–18, 22–23; Williams's
appointment, 22
Louisiana: lynching (1946), 57; slave
rebellion (1811), 49. *See also* New
Orleans riots
Ludlow, Colorado: Massacre, 82–84
Lyman, Theodore, Jr., 31, 46, 47
Lynching, 2, 53–54, 56–57, 142;
attempts, 46, 101; occurrences of,
32, 38, 40, 51, 57, 106, 107, 109

MacArthur, Douglas, 125, 127, 129
Mackintosh, Ebenezer, 94, 95
Madison, James, 103, 104
Mann, Woodrow, 14
Marshall, Thurgood, 56
"Martian Invaders" riots, 144–46
Massachusetts: Shays's Rebellion,
9–12; Palmer Raids, 41. *See also*
Boston riots
McFarlane, James, 97

McGee, Wilson, 148
Media, 153–154. *See also* Press;
Radio; Television
Mexican-Americans, 54
Milwaukee, Wisconsin: streetcar
workers' strike, 72
Minneapolis, Minnesota: attack on
City Hall (1934), 72; labor riot
(1934), 72
Minority groups, 41–42, 156. *See also*
by group
Mitchell, John, 113
Mob: definition of, 1–3; psychology of,
3, 4–5, 41–42, 113, 143, 149–150, 154
Mondello, Keith, 61–62
Montana "Strangler" mobs, 142
Moseley, George Van Horn, 124, 125
Movie riots, 149–50
Moynihan, Daniel Patrick, 5

National Commission on the Causes
and Prevention of Violence, 87
National Guard: and campus
violence, 137; Chicago (1968), 84;
Detroit (1917), 51, (1967), 131–32;
Kent State (1970), 111–13; Little
Rock (1957), 13; Newark (1967),
130–31; racism of, 130, 131–32;
rioting by, 51, 111–13, 130, 131;
strikebreaking, 76, 82; Washington,
D.C. (1968), 134
National Labor Relations Board
(NLRB), 74
Native American party. *See* "Know-
Nothings"
Neville, John, 97
New Deal, 73–74, 77, 129
New Orleans riots, 49, 118–119; 120
New York City: Bensonhurst (1989),
60–62; "body-snatching" riot
(1788), 141–42; cab drivers' strike,
72; Crown Heights riot, 155; riot

(1863), 104–9; flour riot (1837), 65–66; hard-hat riot (1970), 113–14; Harlem (1935), 144; Howard Beach (1986), 61; King verdict (1992), 20; police riot (1874), 79–81; police riot (1988), 81–82; slave rebellion (1712), 48–49

Newark, New Jersey: Civil War draft riots, 109; six-day riot (1967), 130–31

Nixon, Richard: election of, 88, 110; invasion of Cambodia, 110–11; and suppression of dissent, 111, 113, 114, 135, 138

Nonviolent protest, 1, 133, 134, 135, 138, 156, 157

Norton, John, 147

O'Connell, J. D., 119

Oklahoma: vigilantes, 110

Olney, Richard, 69

Opdyke, George, 108

Operation Rescue, 23–24, 157

Palmer raids, 40–41

Palmer, A. Mitchell, 39, 40–41

Patterson, John, 60

Patton, George, 125, 127

Peck, Jim, 59

Pennsylvania: election riot (1742), 150; Whiskey Rebellion, 96, 97. *See also* Philadelphia; Pittsburgh

Perry, Lucia, 111–112

Pew, Thomas, Jr., 87

Philadelphia, Pennsylvania: cab drivers' strike, 72; Whiskey Rebellion, 98

Phillips, Floyd, 70

Pinkerton detectives, 68

Pittsburgh, Pennsylvania: Whiskey Rebellion, 97

Police: and antilabor activities, 41, 68, 69, 72, 74–75, 76, 79–81, 82, 83; on campuses, 136, 137; crowd control, 3, 5, 122, 134, 147; excessive force of, 1, 5, 76, 88, 118–19, 130, 131; excessive restraint of, 5, 17, 19, 20, 38, 39, 54, 55, 58, 59–60, 114, 115; injured by mob violence, 66, 71, 100, 105, 106, 124, 130, 138, 148; and media, 80, 87, 153; public perception of, 21, 88, 114–15; and racism, 14, 20, 22, 51, 54, 55, 56, 58, 59–60, 88, 132; role of, 3; training of, 3, 5, 20, 22, 134. *See also* "Law and order" crackdowns; Los Angeles Police Department; Police brutality; Police riots

Police brutality, 3, 20, 21, 56, 88, 118–19; charges of, 17–18, 51, 76, 82, 87, 88, 119; occurrences of, 17, 51, 55, 72, 80, 81–82, 83, 85–88, 106, 124, 130, 132, 137, 138; rumors of, 21, 131, 144; toleration of, 17, 20, 51–52, 80–81, 84, 87–88

Police riots, 3, 115; Chicago (1968), 84–87; Ludlow (1914), 83; New Orleans (1866), 118–19; St. Louis (1917), 51; Tompkins Square Park (1874), 79–80, (1988), 18–82

Pontiac, Michigan: busing riot, 16

"Port Huron Statement," 135

Poverty, 5–6, 21–22, 58, 67, 70–71, 82, 132–33

Press: abolitionist press, 45, 46, 48, 105, 118; allaying violence, 20, 87; bias, 153; and Bonus Army, 121, 123, 126, 127, 129; censorship of, 39, 48, 76, 87, 118; and Chicago police riot, 85, 86, 87; and corporations, 68, 75, 80; and Frank trial, 37–38; inflaming violence, 19,

Press: inflaming violence (*continued*)
40, 54, 61, 153; and King verdict
riots, 17, 18, 19, 20, 153; polls by, 18,
22, 23, 88; public response to, 88,
153; racist propaganda, 37–38, 55;
and social change, 57, 66; violence
against, 14, 59, 61, 85, 87, 103,
105–6
Preston, Thomas, 91, 92
Propaganda, 27, 31, 37, 38, 39, 50, 55,
93
Proprietary party, 150
Psychology of mobs, 3, 4–5, 41–42,
113, 143, 148, 149–50, 154, 156
Pullman strike, 67–70
Pullman, George, 67, 68

Quakers, 150

Rabble-rousers, 1, 13. *See also*
Samuel Adams; Tom Watson
Race riots, 49, 50, 154; Alabama
(1961), 59–60; Chicago (1919),
52–53, (1951), 57–58; Crown
Heights (1991), 155; Detroit
(1943), 54–56; East St. Louis
(1917), 50–52; Harlem (1935),
144; Hawkins murder (1989),
60–62; Little Rock (1957), 13–15;
Newark (1967), 130–31; New
Orleans (1866), 118–19; New York
(1863), 106–9; Pontiac (1971), 16;
summer 1968, 134–35; World War I
era, 50, 52, 53–54; zoot-suit
riots, 54
Racism, 33, 34, 36, 50, 56, 57, 61, 62,
130, 155; and courts, 23; and law
enforcement agencies, 14, 20, 21,
51, 54, 55–56, 59–60, 88, 130–32;
and legislation, 34, 35, 36, 118, 119;

and politicians, 13–15, 34, 35, 36,
37–38, 50, 57; and violence, 2, 3, 5,
48, 57, 61, 144, 154; and white flight,
58. *See also* Race riots
Radio, 55, 144–45, 129, 153
Railroads: American Railway Union,
67; B&O railroad and Bonus Army,
121; Central Pacific Railroad,
34; and Chinese labor, 34, 35;
General Managers Association,
68; Pullman Company, 67;
Pullman strike, 67–70; Union
Pacific, 34
Rap music, 146–47
Reconstruction, 50, 118–20
Red-baiting, 75, 99, 114, 129. *See also*
Communism: fear of
Redcoats. *See* British troops
Reno, Milo, 99
Republicans, 74, 119, 120, 122
Republic Steel strike riot, 74–76
Revere, Paul, 93
Revolution, 11; definition of, 2;
fear of, 39, 40, 66, 83–84, 122,
124. *See also* American Revolution
Revolutionary War, *See* American
Revolution
Ribicoff, Abraham, 87
Richardson, Elliot, 113
Riots: causes of, 2–6, 41–42, 53, 58,
76–77, 101, 115, 132–33, 143, 144,
147, 148–49, 149–50, 154, 156;
definition of, 1–2; prevention of, 4,
5, 6, 22, 156–57
Rock concert riots, 146–147
Rock Springs, Wyoming: anti-Chinese
riots, 35
Roe v. Wade, 23
Romney, George, 131, 132
Roosevelt, Franklin D., 73, 100, 129
Roosevelt, Theodore, 36, 69, 142
Rosenbaum, Yankel, 155

Rubenstein, Richard E., 156
Rumors, 56, 144; instances inciting violence, 21, 27, 54, 55, 57, 61, 144, 150; and *War of the Worlds,* 145
Russian Revolution (1917), 39, 40

Saenz, Delia S., 148–49
St. Louis, Missouri: election-day riot (1854), 31–32, 150–51; pool integration riot, 57; Woodrow Wilson speech, 110
San Francisco, California: anti-Chinese violence, 32; King verdict riots (1992), 20
Sanford, Edward, 107
Savio, Mario, 136
Sayre, Nora, 86
Scalawags, 119
Scapegoats, 106, 154
Seattle, Washington: anti-Chinese, 35–36; Depression (1933), 72; King verdict (1992), 20
Segregation, 13, 15, 16, 53, 57, 59–60
Seigenthaler, John, 59
Sharpton, Reverend Al, 61
Shays, Daniel, 9, 10
Shays's Rebellion, 9–13
Simi Valley, California: 18, 20, 22
Singer, Melanie, 22
Slavery, 3; emancipation, 48, 50, 119; North and, 48, 49; rebellions: 48–49, 117–18. *See also* Abolition
Smith, Darrell C., 75–76
Smith, Gerald L. K., 55
Smith, Margaret Bayard, 143
Social Security, 71, 73–74
Socialism, 69–70, 73, 74
Sons of Liberty, 92
Soon Ja Du, 155
Soule, Frank, 33

South Carolina: antiabolitionist laws, 118; slave rebellion, 49
South End mob, 94, 95–96
Southern Tenant Farmers Union (STFU), 73
Speech: freedom of, 114. *See also* First Amendment rights
Sports fans violence, 147–49
Stamp Act Congress, 94
Stevenson, Adlai E., 58
Strikebreakers, 33, 50, 53, 68, 74, 105
Strikes, 39, 72, 81, 109; Colorado miners, 82–84; East St. Louis (1917), 50–51; Farm Holiday, 99–101; GM, 74; Pullman (1894), 67–69; Republic Steel, 74–76; student strikes, 112, 136
Stringfellow, William, 132
Students: alienation, 88, 135–36; protests, 110–15, 135–38; perception of police, 114–15; public perception of, 88, 113, 115, 138; Students for a Democratic Society, 135–38
Sullivan, L. B., 60

Tacoma, Washington: anti-Chinese riots, 35
Taxation: American Revolution, 93–96; as cause of protest, 3, 93, 157; Farm Holiday, 99, 100; Shays's Rebellion, 10; Whiskey Rebellion, 96–98
Television, 153; and Chicago police riot, 85–86, 87, 88; and King verdict riots, 17, 19, 20, 22; and Montgomery Freedom Riders riot, 59
Thomas, Norman, 73
Thompson, George, 45

Toledo, Ohio: autoworkers' strike, 72; draft riots, 109

Truman, Harry S, 57

Turner, Nat, 117–18

Tyler, Nancy, 146

U.S. Commission on Industrial Relations, 83

UAW (United Automobile Workers Union), 74

Unemployment, 21, 65–66, 79, 80, 130

Unions: African-Americans and, 50–51, 53, 105, 119; ARU, 67–68; Chinese labor and, 33, 35; Colorado miners' strike, 82–84; IWW, 39, 40, 41; Pullman strike, 67–69; recognition of, 74, 76–77, 84; Republic Steel strike, 74–76; STFU, 73; struggle to organize, 67–68, 72–74; UAW/CIO, 74. *See also* Strikebreakers; Strikes

Ursuline Convent riot, 27–31, 154; anti-Catholic prejudice, 27, 154; casualties, 30; Louisa Goddard account of, 28–29; repercussions, 31; rumors and, 27, 28, 30

Veterans: African-American, 53–54, 56–57; American Revolution, 9, 10; World War I Bonus Army, 120–29

Vicksburg, Mississippi: gambling riots, 142

Vietnam War, 88, 110–11; opposition to, 84–86; 110–14, 136–138

Vigilantes: and abolition, 45–48; definition of, 2, 142; and Exclusion Act, 35–36; and Frank case, 37–38; and ghetto riots (1968), 134–35; Montana "Strangler" mobs, 142;

Vicksburg gambling riots, 142; during World War I, 39–40, 109–10

Virginia: Nat Turner's rebellion (1831), 117, 118; and *War of the Worlds* (1938), 145; and Whiskey Rebellion (1794), 97

Voting rights, 33, 50, 119–20. *See also* Election-day riots

Wagner Labor Relations Act, 74, 77

Walker Report, 87

War of 1812, 103–4

War of the Worlds, 144. *See also* "Martian Invaders" riots

Washington, D.C.: Bonus Army (1932), 120–29; Jackson inauguration (1829), 143; King assassination riot (1968), 133–34

Washington, George, 11, 12, 93, 97–98

Watson, Thomas E., 37, 38

Watts riots. *See* Los Angeles

Weathermen, 138

Webster, Daniel, 143

Welles, Orson, 144

Wells, H. G., 144

West, George P., 83

Whiskey Rebellion, 96–99

White House: Bonus Army march on, 123, 124; Jackson inauguration, 143

White, Hugh, 91

Williams, Willie, 22

Wilson, Pete, 19, 20, 22

Wilson, William Julius, 22, 58

Wilson, Woodrow, 38–39, 70, 83–84, 110

Wisconsin Farm Holiday, 100

Woo, Michael, 21

Workingmen's party, 34, 35

World War I, 38, 110; domestic
    violence and, 39–40, 50–52,
    109–110; opposition to, 39, 70,
    109; veterans of, 53–54, 120–29
World War II: domestic violence and,
    54–56; veterans of, 56–58

Young, Stephen M., 112

Zoot-suit riots, 54
Zwerg, Jim, 60